DEFIANT
SECOND DAUGHTER

DEFIANT
SECOND DAUGHTER

MY FIRST 90 YEARS

a memoir by
BETTY LEE SUNG

Published by Advantage, Charleston, South Carolina.
Member of Advantage Media Group.

ADVANTAGE is a registered trademark and the Advantage colophon is a trademark of Advantage Media Group, Inc.

Printed in the United States of America.

ISBN: 978-1-59932-610-8
LCCN: 2015952735

This publication is designed to provide accurate and authoritative information in regard to the subject matter covered. It is sold with the understanding that the publisher is not engaged in rendering legal, accounting, or other professional services. If legal advice or other expert assistance is required, the services of a competent professional person should be sought.

 Advantage Media Group is proud to be a part of the Tree Neutral® program. Tree Neutral offsets the number of trees consumed in the production and printing of this book by taking proactive steps such as planting trees in direct proportion to the number of trees used to print books. To learn more about Tree Neutral, please visit www.treeneutral.com. To learn more about Advantage's commitment to being a responsible steward of the environment, please visit www.advantagefamily.com/green

Advantage Media Group is a publisher of business, self-improvement, and professional development books and online learning. We help entrepreneurs, business leaders, and professionals share their Stories, Passion, and Knowledge to help others Learn & Grow.

For my children and grandchildren.

ACKNOWLEDGMENTS

I am grateful to my children and grandchildren for imploring me to leave them a legacy, especially those who chose Jana Murphy and the team at Advantage Media to organize this chronology of my life. I am also grateful to all those who have crossed my path for making my life interesting.

INTRODUCTION

When sleeping women wake, mountains move.
—Chinese proverb

I did not set out to live a rebellious life, to be a defiant daughter, an outspoken author, or an angry activist. In the culture I was born into, all these things were unacceptable.

I did not set out to marry a man who would run off with another woman and leave me to raise our four children on my own. I did not plan to bring up four stepchildren or to discover that as they grew into young men and women, they, like my own children, were one of the great sources of pride and joy in my life. I could not have known that they would one day cause my greatest sorrow.

I did not set out to fight a new fight in my ninth decade. At my age, after what felt like a lifetime of pushing back against oppressive sexism and infuriating, demeaning racism—not because I was looking for a fight but because those were the obstacles that blocked my path—I was ready for a more quiet life. But I was too trusting, and I have since learned that the elderly, too, are vulnerable and that we, too, must learn to speak up and fight for what is right.

Looking back, I see now that I had a front row seat for many of the great and terrible events of the 20th century and that those events are intertwined with my experiences and the choices I've made.

Those moments in history have framed my path through life so far, a path that has been marked with my enduring contributions—my children, my books, my research, and my legacy as one of the first professors of Asian American history in the United States.

I was an angry young woman when I wrote my first book, *Mountain of Gold*—so much so that I announced it in the very first

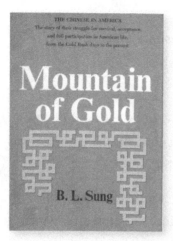

line. I was outraged at the racist portrayals of Chinese people that I'd found at every turn up to that point in my life, and I wanted to do something about it. After that book was written, I was still driven, but I also had a good life. I was respected, with a career that I believed to be important, a husband who loved me and was proud of me, and children who were successfully finding their own ways in the world.

First book, published 1967.

I am an angry woman again as I sit down to write this book. I have lost a great deal in recent years—both worldly things, which I can live without, and more vital aspects of my life. I have had to give up my relationship with my husband of four decades and with the four stepchildren that I raised for 37 years. I have seen the end of a remarkably long run of good health.

I hope the process of writing my story will help me to accept the things that are beyond my power to change and to embrace all that is still good in my life. I am blessed with my four children and six grandchildren. I still remember the events of my life vividly. I have a quick mind and the ability to write. In these pages, I hope I can call on these gifts to tell the story of how this defiant second daughter grew up to live a rebellious, principled, and meaningful life.

Chapter 1

ABOVE THE LAUNDRY

Many years ago, when I was tracing my genealogy, I was able to follow my father's lineage in the Lee clan for generations. In each village, there is an ancestral hall where the plaques of all the males in a family are hung. In my father's village, this record of the men's lineage goes back for thousands of years.

My mother's history is not so clear. I know her family name was Chin, but in Chinese custom, once a woman marries, she leaves her family and village and loses her identity to her groom's. There are no plaques tracing generations of Chinese women in the ancestral halls. For centuries, the Chinese culture did not find the records of its daughters worthy of keeping. Because of this, the genealogy of my mother's side of the family is lost to me.

In my life, unequal treatment and incomplete records seem to have become recurring themes. Perhaps it all started with my father's long and well-documented family history and my mother's mysteriously blank ancestry.

CঙৎO

My father was only 18 years old in 1909 when he and my mother were married in a match arranged by their families. Just days later, he traveled, alone, on the ship *Korea* from China to the United States, while she stayed behind. He was following in the footsteps of countless Chinese men who'd shipped off to make their fortunes in America since 1848, when merchant ships first began putting into Canton with sailors who told wild tales of great mountains of gold in California. The Gold Rush was long over by 1909, but thousands of men had since managed to get to the United States and make their fortunes—and in the process they had brought honor to their families and sent home hard-earned wages that allowed their parents, spouses, and children to live well.

My father settled in Washington, D.C. and opened a hand laundry business. Running a laundry was one of the few career avenues available to an uneducated man who could not speak English but who was willing to spend long hours at a dirty job few others were eager to accept. For 11 years, my father worked and saved until he finally accumulated enough money to go back to China and get his wife in 1921. I have wondered what she imagined her life in the United States would be like as she made the long journey by ship and then by train from Toishan, China, to America's capital city with the husband she hardly knew. I doubt she fully understood that she was about to begin a very lonely and hard life, given the status she had enjoyed as the wife of a *guest of the Gold Mountain.*

After they were reunited, my parents had five children—Rose, Milton, Joe, Homer, and me. I was the third child and the second daughter, born in October 1924.

As the youngest girl, I always knew I was the least important person in our family. A Chinese daughter is expected to be obedient above all other things, and countless proverbs reflect this ideal. There is a Confucian tenet known as the Three Followings, and the concept is simply that a woman should submit herself to the dictates of first her father, then her husband, and then her eldest son. Thus, throughout her life, she is subservient to a man—and often more than one. This thinking, inspired by Confucian teachings, influenced the perceptions of the Chinese for over 2,000 years, so it was typical that my parents would look at me as less important—and even perhaps less a part of the family—than my brothers. After all, a daughter is eventually married off, and at that point she becomes, for all intents and purposes, a part of her husband's family of origin and no longer a part of her own.

Even though I was aware of my place in the family and of what was expected of me from a very young age, I was not very accepting of my fate. I was noisier, more full of questions, and less obedient than my sister in all things. At times, I was more defiant than my brothers—though we were all, by most standards, very well behaved. I did not *feel* less important, and I found it difficult to act so.

The things I remember most about my mother are that she was always sick and that she, more than anyone else, made me feel that I was on the lowest rung of the family. She had been raised to believe that girls existed mostly to wait on the opposite sex, and she accepted this and did what she could to perpetuate it. My sister Rose and I had little value of our own. Our daily lives reflected this bias in every way. Even when we were small, we were expected to pick up after our brothers and make their beds. We were expected to do our chores, keep our heads down, and do as we were told. In everything from household chores to sleeping arrangements to the allotment of food, Rose and I were last. If my mother cooked a fish for dinner, she would make two dishes—one with the head and tail for the girls and one with the choice pieces of meat for the boys. She did the same with meats and poultry.

Even as a small child, I'd try to take my food from the dish with the choicer meat, but Mother would hit me with her chopsticks every time. I think she must have hit me every single day.

The way my mother treated my sister and me reflected all she had ever known and learned about the value of girls. Looking back, I'm sure it also reflected her disillusionment with her own life. She was illiterate but intelligent and stranded in a country where she was isolated and looked down on. She was young but weak with arthritis and allergies, and she had five young children to care for and mountains of other people's dirty clothes and linens to attend to every day. As was typical in a Chinese family, her relationship with my father was very reserved, and it is difficult to believe she found much solace in her marriage. I don't ever remember seeing my parents touch one another. They rarely spoke. I never even heard him call her by her name. He referred to her as "Milton's mother" when he wanted her attention. For most of my life, I did not even know her given name.

My sister Rose is three years older than I, and she was my constant childhood companion. We shared a bed together for the first ten years of our lives, and we worked together in the kitchen and in the laundry. Rose managed to get us a couple of 5-cent porcelain dolls, and we played with them together when we had time.

Rose and I were as different as two little girls could be. When I was defiant, she was compliant. When I disrupted our family life with my questions or my ideas about being treated as well as my brothers, Rose did what she could to keep the peace. I tried to test my mother's limits every day, and Rose tried to be a helpmate to her. Rose was always the smallest of the siblings, but despite her size and being a girl, she was the boss among us kids, and we all knew it. I didn't mind being bossed around by Rose very much. Even when we were very young, I think I knew that she was the one person I could always depend on.

೦ফ৪ফ

The first home I remember is our house on Pennsylvania Avenue in Washington, D.C. We were only about four miles from the White House, though it was a world away from our day-to-day life. I remember running up and down the steps of the Capitol building with my sister and brothers one day, though we would never have attempted to enter that imposing building. At the time, there was no obvious security around the building—not at all like it is today.

My parents ran the laundry business on the first floor of our house, and our family lived in the three rooms above, though only two of those rooms were heated. Our little kitchen had a gas stove and an icebox that required a large block of ice every other day. It was my duty to go to the icehouse, buy the block, and haul it home in a red wagon. As ice melted in the icebox, I had to empty the pan beneath to keep it from overflowing. It was not until I was an adult that I had an electric refrigerator.

Our home was tiny, and we had very few belongings. We did not have toys or decorations or fancy clothes, but we always had enough food to eat, shoes on our feet, and coats in the winter.

My father was stern and distant, a typical Chinese father of the time. We respected him, never talked back, and always did as he commanded—or else we suffered swift and effective punishment. If we disobeyed him, he would grab us by the legs, turn us upside down, and spank us. He was very strong, and the spanking hurt. I don't think he was especially cruel; the kind of discipline he used to keep us children in line was just like the discipline most other Chinese fathers used. Parental authority was absolute, and any misbehavior on the part of the children reflected terribly on the parents. When a Chinese child behaves badly, other people in the community don't comment on the child's naughtiness. Instead they say, "*Mo kao fen,*" which translates to mean "no training." No parent wanted to claim children who were poorly trained!

To be safe, since I was already the least favored child in our family, I stayed out of my father's way as much as I could.

My father's routine was as consistent as the sun. Every day, he rose at 6:00 a.m., and we children got up, too. Father made coffee in a saucepan on the stove, and we ate bread for breakfast. Rose packed our lunches for school—a sandwich, a pastry, and a piece of fruit for each of us.

While we were at school, my father worked, listening to the radio while he went about his labors. The first floor was taken up by ironing boards, sinks, shelves for clean bundles, a huge washing machine, and a drying room. From 6 a.m. to 10 p.m., six and a half days a week, for more than 40 years, my father toiled—sorting dirty clothes, washing them, ironing them, and putting them into bundles. At the turn of the century, an estimated seven in ten ethnic Chinese men in the eastern United States worked in a laundry.

When I was a girl, it cost ten cents to have a shirt cleaned and pressed and eight cents for a sheet. There was no such thing as wrinkle-free clothing. Every item that was washed had to be ironed by hand. When I was little, my siblings and I used six-pound irons heated over an open flame. My father used an eight-pound iron. There was no air conditioning in the house, and summer days in the laundry were stifling.

It was a great relief to all of us when we switched to electric irons—they were much easier, and cooler, to handle. I don't recall ever burning myself, but throughout my childhood, my hands were rough and calloused from the wear of the iron.

After school every day, my siblings and I ironed shirts until 7:00 p.m. When it got close to mealtime, my father would go to the cash register, take out a few dollars, and tell us to go to the store to buy what he wanted for dinner. My mother was a wonderful cook, and so was my father. As far as I could tell, his sole enjoyment in life was good food. He always had a bowl of rice whiskey or rice wine before dinner and then two bowls of rice with his evening meal. He never ate leftovers, so every meal was freshly cooked, with exactly enough for that sitting and no extra.

Each member of our family had a bowl, chopsticks, and a spoon. Those were our only utensils. I don't remember there ever being a fork in the house. We searched for one in vain when Rose's Sunday school teacher came for a visit. It wasn't until I went to college that I learned to eat with one.

Despite the fact that I often got hit with chopsticks, our dinners were always a quiet affair. My parents rarely spoke—to us or to one another. After dinner, my siblings and I did homework, and my father resumed his laundry work. Every night at 10:00, the lights were out.

CR&O

On Sunday afternoons, my father would put on his only suit and go to Chinatown, where the Chinese families had in many ways created a pseudo government for their own people. In Chinatowns all over America, organizations had been set up to help facilitate the business of daily life for Chinese immigrants. At the lowest level, there was the village *fong,* a gathering of men from one native village in China in their new city. Members like my father would come together every Sunday to sit and chat, greet new arrivals, exchange news or gossip, and sometimes play cards or *pai-gau.* The *fong* had rooms for guests or those who were temporarily out of work to sleep and cook meals. Many Chinese used the *fong's* address as their mailing address and would pick up their mail on Sundays.

The next level of organization after the *fong* was the family association. There are hundreds of millions of Chinese people in the world, but there are only 438 traditionally recognized surnames. As they arrived in the United States, many newcomers chose to settle near others with their same family name, and so there were predominant families in each major city, including the Moys in Chicago, the Yees in Pittsburgh, and in Washington, my father's family, the Lees.

The family association offered room and board to those who needed it and opportunities to socialize with one's kinsmen, but it also offered some social supports. The association helped those in its group who needed help finding services like a medical provider or an interpreter. It also operated its own credit union and had a panel of elders who were trusted to help resolve any disputes between members. The expenses of these associations were paid through payments from the men who were members—much like dues to a union or club.

Every week, my father served for two hours as the money overseer and dispenser in his association's credit union. None of the Chinese families we knew back then ever used—or even set foot inside—an American bank. It was just as well, as no bank of the time would have loaned to a Chinese person anyway. To serve the purpose of a bank, each person in the credit union with a share contributed $10 each week. If a person needed to borrow a lump sum—usually $1,000—he would bid for the money and then pay a higher deposit to the credit union each week to pay the debt. Because my father was trustworthy and respected, the credit union elected him to collect and dispense its funds. He had only been educated through the fourth grade, but he was an intelligent and honest man, and he was able to keep the credit union's books.

My father also served on the panel of elders for his association, and he took his role of helping to keep the peace in his group seriously. Just as a Chinese family does all it can to keep any problems, failures, or weaknesses hidden within the family, the association does all it can to confine disputes within the village group or the family organization to avoid the shame of having its private difficulties exposed to the world.

Typical differences between members included wrangling over debts, businesses that were perceived as interfering with one another, and occasional family disputes. I remember hearing of one case concerning a wife who wanted to send money to her father back in China, but her husband would not agree. The woman argued that since she worked side-by-side with her husband every single day in their laundry business, she should be able to send a gift to her father if she liked. The husband argued that since they had married, his wife was a part of *his* family alone and they had no obligation to her family of origin.

The panel sided with the husband. Their judgments almost always reflected the traditional roles and values of ancient Chinese society. Even though the panel had no authority of enforcement, their opinions were respected—and usually obeyed.

Some Sundays, my father would take the family along to Chinatown, usually leaving Rose and me with our mother at the home of another Chinese family to visit. This was my mother's only social outing of the week.

On Sunday evening, Father would come home after having dinner with the men of his *fong*, hang up his suit, and prepare to start his long work week again. All his life, I only remember him owning that one suit.

CB&O

Even though we children went to school, in every other aspect of our lives we were closely insulated within the Chinese community and culture. At home, we only spoke the Toishanese dialect of my father's native region. We never went to the movies, to non-Chinese restaurants, to the swimming pool, or to a doctor or dentist. If you got sick in our household, you either recovered or died.

In part, our insulated life was dictated by the demands of my father's business. The laundry required a huge time commitment from every member of our family to continue to operate. But there were other factors in our isolation, as well. The Americans all around us were an unknown quantity, and we were never certain whether we would be welcome in public places or businesses that were American-owned. Certainly there were places where we would have been turned away. We had heard stories of Chinese people being mercilessly persecuted in other parts of the country in the past, and we were careful to keep to ourselves. I don't remember ever being invited to play after school or on the weekend with any of my classmates from school, but I did not invite anyone to my home, either.

We never celebrated American holidays, not even Christmas. The only holiday we celebrated was Chinese New Year. Then, my Mother would make tons of pastries, and it seemed like every Chinese person in Washington would descend upon our house to eat them. As children, we all got *hung bao,* or *lay see,* red envelopes with a quarter or nickels or dimes. I remember my parents always gave us children gold coins, which they confiscated at the end of the day.

CRCR

By 1933, the Depression in the United States was so severe that my father found it nearly impossible to support his family of five children on the meager income from the laundry. Compounding his problems was my mother's constant illness and her dissatisfaction with her life in America. She worked from dawn to dusk, but her joints ached, she was always tired, and she missed being around people with whom she could converse and relax.

Finally, my father booked passage to China for all seven members of our family on the ship the *President Jackson*, leaving from Seattle on March 12, 1934. I was nine years old, and although I would one day return to Washington and the Pennsylvania Avenue laundry, neither my family nor my life would ever be the same after our voyage back to my father's village in Toishan.

Family photo, 1935. Joe, Milton,
Father, Homer, Rose, Betty.

CؖۛؖBO

Chapter 2

LIFE IN CHINA

When we arrived in China, we were quickly raised in status from the family of a poor laundryman to a class known as *guests of the Gold Mountain*. Ours was one of the many families who had done well by going to America, and my father was respected for his accomplishments. His hard-earned American money was worth far more in China than it was in the United States, and he built us a three-story house in Toishan City, a county seat at the mouth of the Pearl River. He enrolled all of us in Chinese school.

Boys and girls went to separate schools in China, and only those whose families could afford to pay were able to go. Students were separated not by age but by what they knew and how many years they had already attended. The curriculum was rigorous—I remember studying algebra in the fourth grade. For me, school was fun. I loved to learn and was looked up to as a leader in my class.

There was a public library near our home with a few shelves of books to lend, and I believe I read every one of them. The habit carried over when I came back to the United States, and for years I went to the public library every Saturday and checked out four books to read during the week.

My mother's life should have been easier after our return to China. She no longer had to work 12-hour-days in the laundry, and she had neighbors and relatives to socialize with. We had relatives in Toishan and nearby, so there was a network of help if she needed it. However, she continued to suffer illness and allergies and painful swelling in her joints. To try to ease her suffering, my father went to a market and bought snake meat for her to eat. The use of snake meat and snake bile in traditional Chinese medicine can be traced back thousands of years. It is still sometimes used today in the hopes of alleviating rheumatoid arthritis pain, but the day after my mother ate this meat, a white film developed over her eyes. She lost much of her sight. This was the first of a number of herbal and traditional medicines that seemed to further damage her health instead of making her better. She believed the promises of every medicine man she met, but even as she tried one potion after another to alleviate her symptoms, she continued to become weaker and sicker.

After a few months with us in Toishan, my father had to return to his laundry business in Washington. He hired a woman to take care of Mother and left on his return ship with my brother Joseph. The rest of us—Rose, Milton, Homer, and I—stayed with our mother.

Left alone with us and in terrible health, my mother became increasingly ill-tempered. She was even more so with me than she was with the boys or Rose. She blatantly favored them. She gave my brothers money to buy sweets from street vendors and bought Milton a bicycle, but she withheld all she could from us girls. She routinely made us wait on the boys, wash their clothes, and do their bidding. When I protested, Mother said, "You must learn how to serve men, and eventually you will serve your husbands." When I balked, she swatted me with a feather duster.

Rose tried to make things easier for our mother by doing what she was told, but I was defiant. To show Mother I could not accept being whipped for not serving my brother, I ran away.

I was lucky, because she sent someone to look for me and bring me home. After that, she tried to treat me more gently.

In 1937, after years of encroachment into a China that was divided between Nationalists and Communists, the Japanese launched a full-scale attack on China that began the Sino-Japanese War, also known as the War of Resistance. The opposing factions of the Chinese government pulled together to fight against their aggressor, but the Japanese soldiers used brutal tactics to take the key Chinese ports. In Toishan, we learned that the Japanese had occupied Shanghai and Nanking, then the nation's capital. We heard about the atrocities that had been committed in Nanking, where hundreds of thousands of civilians were slaughtered and thousands of women of all ages were raped. As the Japanese defeated larger portions of China, their attacks began moving closer to Toishan. Our city was a target for two reasons: It was the origin of most of the Chinese who had emigrated overseas and so possessed more wealth than many cities, and it was the endpoint of a railroad that ran to Chiangmen, across the river from Canton. The Japanese military coveted control of the railroad for the iron in its tracks.

Over the course of 1938, the Japanese bombers came closer and closer to us. I still remember the sound of the air raid sirens and how we would all run to shelters in the mountains that were supposed to be safe. Someone had dug great holes into the mountainside for these shelters, but some of the man-made caves were bombed anyway, and the people inside were annihilated.

In the midst of the raids and our fears for the future of Toishan and China, our family suffered a tragedy. My mother prepared a soup from some kind of wild animal and special herbs and gave it to my brothers Milton and Homer. We girls were denied that soup. Homer became terribly sick after this, and he died. Rose tells me that Homer died of pneumonia, but I don't remember him being sickly, except after he drank that soup. He was seven years old.

My mother, already ill and depressed, was deeply affected by Homer's death. Her own health took a turn for the worse after he was gone.

I was barely 12, and when the bombings became more frequent, my mother sent me to our home village where an aunt lived to keep me out of harm's way. She kept Rose behind to care for her. While I was in my aunt's village, we didn't experience the daily bombings, although the village was just four *li* (1.25 miles) from Toishan City. We could see the Japanese planes—we could sometimes even see the pilots in the cockpits because they flew so low.

In the village where I stayed, most of the people were women, elderly, or children. Many men had gone abroad to earn money to send home. Left behind, the women grew their vegetables and crops, picked fuel up in the mountains, and lived a daily life pretty much like that of their ancestors from centuries before. I helped where I could. I went with the women to cut firewood and grasses to burn and to harvest peanuts and sweet potatoes. Because I was from the United States, the women made allowances for me, making my loads lighter than those they carried themselves.

At mealtimes, I used to trade my bowl of white rice for someone else's sweet potatoes. My aunt used to laugh at me for doing so. Most of the farmers could not afford white rice; they ate sweet potatoes for bulk instead. A bowl of white rice was a treat for them, and there was no shortage of people willing to trade with me.

When school started, I was sent back to Toishan City, and that's when I really experienced the daily raids. At first, my brother, Milton, looked upon them as a lark. He'd get on his bicycle and take off, picking up pieces of bomb shrapnel to keep for souvenirs. Rose, then 15, took a very different tack and hid under the bed. I can't remember exactly how I reacted—only that I was terrified.

My mother had been sick for most of her life, but Homer's death gravely affected her, and it was only a few months after his passing that she died. She was only 46 years old.

I remember all of us children lying on the floor in front of her corpse, listening as professional mourners sang the traditional chants. I didn't understand the rituals at all. I just did as I was told. I had never felt close to my mother, but I thought about the sorrow of her life. She had been separated from her husband for 11 years, only to finally go to the United States and find her role was to wash other peoples' dirty clothes from dawn to dusk each day. She had borne five children in nine years, all the while aching with pain. She had returned to her homeland only to lose first her eyesight and then her youngest son.

Our aunts from the village came to stay with us, but it was Rose who made the decisions about how to handle my mother's passing and what to do next. From the day my mother died until we eventually found our way back to our father, she was the default head of our fragmented little family.

CROB

In May of 1938, the Japanese army decided to take southern China. First, they tried to soften up the territory with bombs, and then they sent in gunboats. We had some news of villages they burned as they neared us. As the soldiers got closer, we could hear the guns from Kwanghai, only a few *li* away. This was not the kind of air raid we had seen before. This was a full-scale attack. Some people were preparing to flee, and Rose announced that we were going back to the United States. My brother Milton and I objected because we would be separated from our friends and schoolmates, but Rose was insistent.

She opened the safe that contained our passports and silver coins—paper money was not yet in vogue. We had some gold coins, too, and Rose sewed those into our pillowcases. She sent Milton to buy train tickets to Canton and then to Hong Kong. I stuffed my pillow into an old suitcase that had no lock, and I insisted on bringing my teddy bear with me. It had been given to me by a lady who sometimes worked in the laundry for my father, and that bear was the only toy I had ever owned. I would not leave without it. I remember running from the bombers when we left with that old suitcase tied up with a sash so it wouldn't fall open and spill my most beloved possession.

Rose, Milton, and I rode the train to Canton, but we had no place to stay when we got there. Japanese planes were actively bombing the city. We made our way to the American consulate, which was closed for the night, and we stood outside the walls there, thinking that the Japanese would be careful not to bomb American property. We leaned against the consulate wall through the entire night, and we survived.

The next day, we managed to get a ride down the Pearl River to Hong Kong, and we met the ticket agent from our village there. He secured third-class passage for us on the *Empress of Asia*, a British ship.

It took 19 days to cross the Pacific, and we shared a room with six other people. We spent our time sitting in a deck area outside our cabin. I was seasick at first, as ships didn't have balancers back then, but after two days I got acclimated to the seas and felt better. Poor Rose was seasick the entire time.

When we finally landed in Seattle, I remember feeling like everything was still moving for days. We had no trouble with the immigration inspectors, because we were all born in the United States, but I was astonished to realize when the inspectors spoke to me that I had forgotten most of the English I'd learned at school in Washington.

Rose managed to get us booked on a train from Seattle to Washington. My father was shocked to see us when we showed up at our Pennsylvania Avenue house on July 4, 1938.

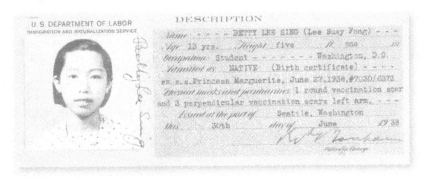

Certificate of Identity given to Betty when she returned to the U.S. She had to carry it around to show she had legitimate right to be in the U.S.

CRLO

I have little doubt that Rose's decision to flee from Toishan saved all our lives. After we left, the bombings eased, and the soldiers arrived. They killed, raped, and maimed men, women, and children from our village and took everything of value they could find. After the initial invasion, they came back periodically, and when they did, the people of Toishan fled into the mountains to hide. As resources were wiped out, another wave of casualties died of starvation. The railroad that had represented the wealth and achievements of Toishan was demolished, both by local Chinese people trying to keep it from the Japanese and by the invading soldiers who wanted to use its iron tracks to make more weapons.

C3 ∞

Chapter 3

A DEFIANT CHOICE

When we came back to the United States, an aunt who had four young children, including twins, asked my father if I could live with her family and help her. I was 13, old enough to be of help, so I moved in with them. The twins, Harry and Jerry, were five. George was six, and Mary was seven. I fed and dressed the twins, took all four children to school, then took them to Chinese school after public school. At home, I helped my aunt and uncle in their laundry and with preparing their meals. After that, I did my own homework. For two years, I lived with them and worked alongside my aunt.

Despite the demanding schedule, the safety and normalcy of this life was a welcome change from the fear I had lived with in China. I loved my school and was even—much to my surprise—elected president of my Hines Junior High School class.

Because my father had his own obligations with the men from his village and the credit union on Sundays, my sister and I were allowed to go the Chinese Community Church on our own each week. About 200 people gathered for the sermon at 2:00 in the afternoon, and our pastor, Dr. C.C. Hung, gave his sermons both in Cantonese and English, one following the other. He preached a unique blend of Methodist, Baptist, and Confucian teachings.

After the service, we stayed for Sunday school. The teachers were incredibly dedicated to us and to other immigrant and American-born Chinese children. They read from the bible and taught lessons from it, but their ministrations went far beyond giving traditional bible lessons. The Sunday school teachers helped those who needed it with their English and spent a great deal of time teaching us how to navigate unfamiliar areas of American culture. They took a personal interest in each of us and even did things like taking us shopping, to the movies, or to the doctor. My Sunday school teacher, Miss Gertrude Barber, was like a mother to me, and Rose's teacher, Mrs. Hannah Dorn, was the same to her. I will always be grateful for the role Miss Barber played in my formative years, and I know there are many other children who would have struggled to assimilate without the kindness and generosity of teachers like her.

Sometimes the young people stayed at church on Sunday evenings, playing ping-pong or badminton or gathering around the piano to sing hymns. Afterwards we would have another brief service and then head home. Those nights out were the biggest social events in our lives.

My father was always waiting up for Rose and me. If we were late, he questioned where we had been. If we didn't give an explanation he considered good enough, he would hit us. He seldom spoke to us, but we were both deathly afraid of him.

CₛƎᏠᎠ

At Eastern High School, where I went next, I found two other Chinese girls, Suen Chin and Lorraine Lee, and we became friends. It was nice to have someone to eat lunch with every day. We seldom interacted with anyone else.

During freshman year, my American History teacher selected me to represent Eastern High in a speech contest extolling the merits of the US Constitution. The principal, however, doubted a Chinese girl could represent his school on such a topic, and he vetoed my selection.

When Rose got married at 19, I was her bridesmaid and helped her sew our dresses. Her new husband, Arthur, was in the restaurant business on Long Island, and so she moved away with him. My father wanted someone to cook for him and told my aunt he needed me at home. I took over cleaning the house and cooking the meals.

My duties included riding the trolley to the K Street market to buy fresh fish, live chickens, and fresh vegetables. It was a strange adventure to ride the trolley home with two live, squawking chickens every other week. My father would kill one chicken and save the other one in the yard for the following week. Even though I didn't have to kill the chickens, I did have to pluck them and chop them.

As it turns out, I was not as good a cook as my mother or father, and my brothers complained about the meals I prepared. Finally, my father told Milton that since I could iron faster than he could anyway, we should trade jobs. From then on, Milton did the cooking, and I ironed every day until dinner.

Later, during World War II, Milton was a soldier stationed at a remote base in Alaska, and his skill in the kitchen proved useful. Many of the other men who'd never learned to cook would pay him to prepare good meals for them.

CR80

During this time, the United States was increasingly at odds with Japan. Despite the way Chinese immigrants had been treated, America had long been a friend to China—and when the Japanese bombed Pearl Harbor in 1941, people in the Chinese community were quietly elated that the United States was joining the war. They would defeat Japan and in doing so ease the suffering of occupied China.

In 1942, when I was 17, I was asked to help with the US war effort. The government wanted to find people who could read and translate Chinese into English. They needed help in creating maps of China that would be legible to US servicemen. Apparently the need was so great, the Army Map Service wanted me to work every afternoon and all day Saturdays on Chinese maps in the Library of Congress. From then on, I went to school from 9 a.m. to 1 p.m. and then took a bus and a streetcar through Washington to the Library of Congress, where I worked on maps from 2 p.m. to 6 p.m. I worked up in the library dome, an area that is now closed to visitors. On warm days, it was stiflingly hot there—easily a hundred degrees.

Our area and its staff were dedicated to Chinese maps. My job was to put an overlay on a map of every place in China and then write the English names on every facet of it, so I would transliterate the characters from the existing map and also indicate what everything was in the area—for example, a bridge, a mountain, a lake, or a village had to be labeled. If the American army wanted to drop into an area, they had to know everything they would find.

I was the youngest girl in the Army Map Service, working alongside adults who were teachers and principals and from all other walks of life. I learned a lot of Chinese from working on those maps and also a lot about the political and physical geography of China. When I didn't recognize a Chinese character, I looked it up and memorized it, and because the translations had to be in the Mandarin dialect, I learned that, too.

I was glad to be helping with the war effort, though I did not have any great understanding of the politics involved. It was just that everyone in the city and the country pulled together in a remarkable way during this time. Everyone wanted to help, and we were all willing to sacrifice to do so. My brothers Milton and Joe both went into the military, and our family, like every other, had to handle the strict rationing of meat, sugar, flour, shoes, stockings, gasoline—so many staples were in short supply. But no one griped about it, because all our hearts were in the war effort.

It was my job at the Library of Congress that got me thinking I might want to go to college. A woman named Cecile Franking was my role model at the Army Map Service. She was half-Chinese and had gone to the University of Michigan. She believed I was smart enough, and she told me how to apply and even helped me fill out applications for scholarships.

I received four acceptance offers. Two were from local universities in Washington. I turned those down because I wanted to go away. I knew it would have been impossible to succeed as a college student while I was still under my father's supervision. The University of

Michigan offered me a second-year scholarship with the option to renew after I proved myself as a freshman, but I needed financial support right from the start. The University of Illinois offered me a full, four-year scholarship—equal to $320 tuition in those days. I accepted their offer and waited eagerly for the end of the school year to come so I could start my new life.

Even though I only went to school half days, my grades were very good, and I qualified as valedictorian of my high school class. This would have been a great honor for me and for my family, but the same principal who had refused to let me compete in the Constitution contest refused to acknowledge me as the top of my graduating class. He chose a white student with similar grades as my replacement, and I was named salutatorian instead.

CR&CO

I had my heart set on going to college, but my father had other plans. He wanted to marry me off to a family that was acceptable to him, just as he had arranged a marriage for my sister. One of the men he chose lived in New York and worked in a *fu joke* (soy bean skin) factory; the other was an unpleasant man whose father owned a thriving restaurant. I did not want to disobey, but I knew I could not marry either one of them.

When I told him I was going to college, he shouted: "Why would any girl be educated?" He couldn't understand—and he did not want to. He felt that my whole life should be serving a husband and bearing children. To our knowledge, no Chinese person, boy or girl, from Washington, D.C. had ever gone away to college. Most people didn't in those days—certainly not the daughters of Chinese laundrymen.

My father said, "If you disobey me, you are no longer my daughter. I will not give you one more penny."

I left home anyway, and he did not speak to me for two years. I wrote him every week, letters in Chinese that told him what I was doing, but he never acknowledged them. After two years, when I wrote and told him I was going to go to a Japanese schoolmate's for Thanksgiving, the thought of me sleeping in the house of the enemy was too much for him. He relented and told me to come home.

I did not know until years later that my father grew to be very proud of me during this time—his daughter actually going to college! My brothers told me he wanted all of Chinatown to know this news. When I made Phi Beta Kappa in my junior year and Milton told him what an honor this was, he was even prouder.

〇З ᐁ

Chapter 4

COLLEGE DAYS

I rode a bus for 18 hours from Washington to Urbana, Illinois, in 1944 with one trunk that contained all my possessions. The clothes in that trunk would last me four years—even after the style changed from short dresses to long ones, my "style" stayed the same. I lived at Lowry Lodge, a girls' student residence a few blocks from campus. Because I was Chinese, the school didn't know where to house me, and so they had settled on this house intended for Jewish girls. I was given room and board in return for washing the lunch and dinner dishes, setting the tables, and keeping the bathrooms clean.

The girls in the Lowry House were amazed at my naiveté, and they'd often sit me down and ask me questions and tell me about life outside my own limited experience. Sometimes I think I learned as much in the lounge of that house as I did in my classes. To me, living in Champaign-Urbana was like being set free. I didn't have to answer to my father, who had demanded work and obedience from me all my life.

At the beginning of my college years, the United States was at war with Japan, Germany, and Italy. Japanese people in the United States were herded into detention camps, even those with American citizenship. Citizens could be released from the camps after two years, and that's how two Japanese American girls came to Chicago and then to the University of Illinois. Their names were Janet Ishihara and Betty Moriwaki. Since no one except Mrs. Lowry would agree to take them (I imagine no one else had agreed to take me either), we all became roommates, sharing one unheated bedroom in the attic.

I have been asked if I resented sharing a room with these Japanese girls because it was Japanese soldiers who had brutalized China and my father's hometown of Toishan City. But I never looked at those two girls and saw my enemies. They were both born in America like I was, and they were both outcasts like I was, too. We became close and long-lasting friends.

Like me, Janet had to work for her room and board, and so we shared the cleaning duties at the boarding house. After a year, the Cosmopolitan Club was organized across town in Urbana, an organization of foreign students from various countries. Janet, Betty, and I were all considered "foreign" (even though we were American citizens), and we were asked if we would rather live in this area. The three of us moved across town together, and Janet and I once again agreed to set tables, wash dishes, and clean bathrooms in exchange for our room and board.

The campus had a contingent of Chinese foreign students who formed the Chinese Student Club. There were exactly 100 of us. Among them were two girls who never dated, one other Chinese American girl who soon dropped out, and me. So when it came to dating, I was more or less the only Chinese American girl on campus.

I was elected the social chairman of the club, and I organized most of our social functions, like picnics, dances, dinner parties, and lectures. Every weekend there were also dances, football games, parties, and other events on campus. Sometimes, I had dates for Friday, Saturday, and Sunday. I had a heavy course load and my chores at the Cosmopolitan Club, but even so, those were the most carefree days of my life.

I was a good student and enjoyed my classes, though at first I struggled with the required English courses in the curriculum. My vocabulary was very limited, and I couldn't even recite the alphabet. We had never spoken English at home, so there were gaps in my understanding of the language. For all these reasons, I was very surprised when an essay I wrote was chosen for publication in the *Green Cauldron*, the freshmen English journal. I was honored to be recognized for my writing—in spite of the fact that I was on academic probation with the university over my shaky English skills.

As I reached a point of having more freedom to choose my courses, I wanted to learn more about Chinese history. The university didn't offer such a class, but after some pestering from me and other students, the administration consented to offer a two-hour course in Asian history. I eagerly signed up but was soon disappointed when I discovered our professor was taking his lecture, word for word, from the *Encyclopedia Britannica*.

During my college career in Illinois, I earned a sociology honors key, a Phi Beta Kappa key, and a Phi Beta Kappa scholarship. I finished my course work in three and a half years, completing a double major in economics and sociology. There was no winter graduation then, so I had to wait until June for my diploma.

CR&D

I was a junior at the university when I met Hsi Yuan Sung. He had been selected among an elite group of students from Southwest United University in China to be sent abroad for special training, and he was studying for his master's degree in economics. He was very smart and had a big, bold personality. After our first date, he claimed me as his girlfriend and threatened anyone who came near me. He had a car—a beat-up jalopy—two new suits, and even a phonograph. He was not wealthy; he was impulsive. He had come to the United States with money exchanged at a favorable rate because he was a top student, but within a year and a half, he had spent it all. After that, his brother had to send him enough money to pay for his university meal tickets.

Hsi Yuan was hard to pronounce, so he took the name William—Bill for short. Bill finished his M.A. from Illinois in a year or so and then left for NYU to pursue his doctorate. Before he left, he proposed, and I agreed to marry him.

On February 22, 1948, Bill Sung and I were married at the Chinese Community Church in Washington, with Rev. C.C. Hung officiating. Rose was my maid of honor. An old friend from the church was a bridesmaid, and my little cousin Mary, whom I had helped raise, was also a bridesmaid.

My father had gone back to Hong Kong, so he was not there for my wedding, but I made my own gown, and Rose and her husband, Arthur, gave a reception and small dinner for Bill and me. We had no money and were very grateful for their generosity.

After the festivities, Bill and I went to New York together to start our new lives.

ᘒ ᘓ

Chapter 5

VOICE OF AMERICA

B ill and I were penniless newlyweds as we started our married
life in a single rented room in Harlem. It was furnished
with a double bed and nothing else. I went to the grocery store and
bought wooden packing crates for ten cents each and used wire to
fashion them into makeshift chairs, a table, and a counter for my
electric cooker. I hung one out the window to serve as a refrigerator
for as long as the weather stayed cold.

I was proud of my handiwork, but we had much bigger problems
to worry about than our lack of furnishings. Bill was still on a student
visa at NYU, so he could not legally work. The little money we had
was running out. Other Chinese students we knew were also struggling, including one who survived for a while on just a quart of milk
a day before he finally went broke, gave up, and went back to China.

Bill was a good student, though, almost finished with his Ph.D.,
and he should have had a bright future. In those days, anyone who
earned an advanced degree in the United States was held in high

esteem in China and was almost assured of a good government position on his return. We could have gone to China when Bill finished his education and lived well there.

What happened next, though, changed everything. In 1949, Mao Tse Tung took power in China and declared the country Communist. The United States immediately severed diplomatic relations with its one-time ally. Chinese students like Bill were forbidden to leave the United States, but they were also forbidden to work. Bill could not go back, yet he could not earn a living, and there would be no more funds coming from his family. We were acquainted with many other young students and immigrants whose funds from China were cut off, leaving them in desperate straits. I knew one young man with a Ph.D. in economics who could only find work as a hatcheck boy and another with an engineering degree who could barely get hired as a dishwasher.

Things went from bad to worse as McCarthyism took hold across the country and everyone of Chinese ancestry was suspected of being Communist. The government even readied the internment camps that the Japanese Americans had just vacated to receive the Chinese Americans if necessary. Mercifully, wiser minds prevailed, and we were never herded into the camps, but government officials continued to try to find a place to lay the blame for "losing China."

To protect ourselves, the Chinese in the United States declared that we were pro-Nationalists, and we wore lapel buttons that proclaimed: "I am Nationalist Chinese."

Merchants in Chinatown dared not import goods or foods from China—only from Taiwan. We flew only the Nationalist flag.

Privately, our feelings about the Communist takeover were more complicated than we could discuss in public. Chiang Kai-shek had run a corrupt government. There had been a great deal of suffering under his rule, and many overseas Chinese and Chinese Americans were hopeful about the new, more egalitarian government taking over. Even as we considered the two very different governments, though, we were hearing reports of the Communist government taking over land, houses, and personal property. We knew there were citizens who had fled China, some of them desperately swimming to Hong Kong—and we knew that some of them had been shot. Shooting those who would escape their government did nothing to boost the new Communist regime in the eyes of the world or in those of the overseas Chinese.

The situation was deeply upsetting to Bill, and occasionally, in his frustration, he would blame me for trapping him in America. As time went on, though, we both realized we might have suffered a far worse fate in China for having been "tainted" by our time in the United States than the hardships we faced in New York. Bill's schoolmates who had returned to China later related how they had been suspected and demoted, how their bank accounts had been seized, and how they had wasted the most potentially productive years of their lives under a haze of distrust.

I could not wait around for Bill, who was limited by his citizenship, to find a way to support us. As soon as I arrived in New York, I started looking for a job. I was an American-born college graduate with a double major and a Phi Beta Kappa key. I was a hard worker and a quick study. I was confident I could get a good job and help keep us afloat.

I was sorely disappointed to discover that as a woman and a Chinese American, I could only find secretarial jobs. At interview after interview, I was asked if I could type and how fast and if I could take shorthand. I had not spent almost four years earning top grades at the university for this, but we needed a source of income, so I took a position as a secretary at a perfume house.

I started the job imagining I'd learn all about the cosmetics industry, then one day open my own factory. The job would be my springboard.

For better or worse, my grand plans were ruined right away. My shorthand was not good enough, and I was fired.

The next job I got was on Wall Street, working as a statistician. As it turned out, companies hired the firm I worked for not to accurately analyze their figures and extrapolate data but to manipulate the figures to make them fit expectations. For each task, I was given a premise and expected to employ the numbers in a way that bore it out. If I couldn't get the numbers to fit, I was told to start over and try again. I was shocked at the dishonesty of the job.

While I was struggling with my conscience and the task of making accounting numbers fit unrealistic objectives, a friend suggested I apply for a job as an announcer at the Voice of America. VOA is the official broadcast institution of the American government around the world. The organization airs news and other programming in English and in dozens of other languages. Back then, it was broadcast mostly through short- and medium-wave radio. Over the years, the government has used the Voice of America to speak directly to citizens of many foreign regions. Though some of the target countries, including Communist China, jammed the signal, the transmissions still managed to reach a wide audience. During the 1950s, Chinese citizens throughout Southeast Asia listened to VOA broadcasts of news, music, and human interest stories.

I was reluctant to apply for the job because my Chinese was not up to par for an announcer, but I went anyway. The director of the Chinese Section, Mr. Jayne, asked if I could write. I told him I hated writing. All through college, I'd opted for oral presentations over written ones whenever possible. For reasons I will never understand, Mr. Jayne asked me to give it a try anyway.

"Write two scripts and show me what you can do," he said. "We need script writers who have a Chinese outlook."

Two weeks later, I returned with the scripts in hand, and he hired me on the spot. Mr. Jayne offered me a salary that was twice what I was making as a statistician, and I was elated to take it.

Colleagues at Voice of America, ca. 1950.

At the time, Voice of America was based in the General Motors Building on 57th Street, so I began working in midtown Manhattan. I was required to write three feature scripts each week. Most of the programming was comprised of newscasts, which announcers translated into the three main Chinese dialects—Mandarin, Cantonese, and Amoy—for the overseas Chinese target audience. My job was to write feature scripts that would capture their interest, and beyond that I could choose subjects that interested me. I thought the people in China and Southeast Asia would have a genuine curiosity about how their compatriots lived and were treated in the country that had long represented the Mountain of Gold. The fact that America was China's enemy at that time just added to the interest.

Initially, I thought these scripts would be easy to write. I would research the activities of Chinese students, workers, and families in America and share what I learned. In reality, the task turned out to be much more challenging. There was almost no published data to be accessed, and the little that existed turned out to be largely inaccurate and overwhelmingly negative. I worked my way from local library branches to some of the best-stocked libraries in the country, but even at the New York Public Library and the libraries at Yale, Princeton, and the Universities of California at Berkeley and Los Angeles, the files were sparse and overwhelmingly racist. Even in the Library of Congress, where House representatives and senators go to seek information to inform the laws they make, I mostly found reports that reinforced stereotypes of the Chinese as cheap laborers, opium smokers, undesirable heathens, and unassimilable aliens, *ad nauseam*.

I struggled not just with my distaste at the derogatory terms and images but with their inaccuracy. These were not my people as I knew them. I had lived in China as a girl, and I had been part of the Chinese community in America all my life. I had witnessed the intelligence, industry, and dignified culture in China. I knew better. Worse yet, I did not just suspect but absolutely knew the terrible injustice these stereotypes caused.

I thought back to the times I'd heard stories of Chinese people who were singled out and intimidated by immigration inspectors. As I rummaged through file after file, looking for useful material to use as inspiration for my human interest stories, I recalled incidents from my own life that had once seemed insignificant. I thought about how my siblings and I, all native-born American citizens, always carried ID papers with us wherever we went—just in case we encountered an immigration inspector. I thought about the day I'd seen Chinese men hurry to hide in the ceiling tiles when a government official came into my father's shop. I remembered my father admonishing me not to share any information with the census taker, because he thought anything I said might be used against us. I thought about the way he had steered our family clear of banks, movie theaters, public pools, doctors, dentists, and even restaurants that he perceived to be only for white Americans.

Everyone I knew in the Chinese community was on some level intimidated by the sense that we were outsiders in America, and the roots of the discrimination that drove that intimidation were laid bare in the inaccurate and often hurtful files I uncovered in libraries across the country.

For their part, the Chinese in America did not actively dispel these negative images. Many of us lived insular lives, reluctant to defy our cultural traditions by speaking out in our defense or arguing our cases. And because there was no one at the time in the Chinese community who did not know someone who had suffered at the hand of the immigration system, people were often suspicious and guarded, sharing only information that could not be kept concealed.

During my first weeks at the Voice of America, I decided to use the opportunity I'd been given to tell the story of my people. I would depict their true history and the myriad ways they were living their lives in America. I would do what I could to raise the profile of the Chinese in America, even if only in translations being broadcast halfway around the world.

Each week, in order to write my program, *Chinese Activities,* I started working to dig up information from original sources. I went to Chinese American communities all over the country, and over time, I began to establish sources who would let me know when something newsworthy was happening in each place.

I studied the history of the American cities with the most significant Chinese populations—Honolulu, San Francisco, and New York—and I observed that there was a pattern of assimilation that was developing more or less from west to east. As each community became home to more generations of people of Chinese descent, the families became more deeply rooted in America and more comfortable with their roles here. At that time, the population of Honolulu was nearly 20 percent Chinese, and many San Francisco Chinese families were having their third and fourth generations of American-born children. That was a big difference from the community where I grew up on the East Coast, where my siblings and most of my peers were the first American-born generation.

I also investigated some of the lesser-known Chinese communities in America, like those in Oakland, Chicago, Phoenix, St. Louis, Baltimore, and Washington. I learned about Chinatowns that continued to thrive, as well as those that had been razed by urban-planning programs or largely left behind by populations that had moved on.

In addition to covering communities and trends, I often wrote profiles of Chinese Americans who'd made great personal or professional accomplishments. One of my profiles was of Toy Len Goon, a woman who emigrated from China with her husband, Dogon Goon, in 1921. In the years that followed, the couple opened a hand laundry in Portland, Maine, and had eight children. When Dogon died in 1941, the children ranged in age from 3 to 16, and Toy Len Goon was left to both run the laundry and raise the children on her own. Miraculously, the family worked together, and each of the eight Goon children became a success in his or her own right. In the end, the family included a doctor, a chemist, a businessman, an engineer, a soldier, and a court reporter. I wrote a profile about Mrs. Goon after she was selected as Maine's Mother of the Year in 1952. She was honored with a parade in New York's Chinatown and a trip to the White House to meet the First Lady.

I often wrote about Chinese immigrants or Chinese Americans who were making an impact in academia, medicine, and the sciences. There was no shortage of stories in this area, and I never tired of countering the stereotypes of unassimilable aliens with those of men and women who were shining stars in their fields. I wrote about Hiram Fong, the son of Chinese immigrants who came to Hawaii to work on the sugar plantations and worked his way through college, then Harvard Law, and eventually to a life of public service. He had played a key role in obtaining statehood for Hawaii.

I wrote about groundbreaking physicists Chen Ning Yang and Tsung Dao Lee, who rewrote the laws of how particles were understood in the 1950s and were lauded by *The New York Times* as having made "the most important development in physics in the past ten years." At just 30, Dr. Lee was the youngest full professor on the faculty at Columbia University when his work was recognized with the Nobel Prize for Physics.

I wrote about doctors, artists, authors, financiers, and Chinese-born architect I.M. Pei, who had been unanimously selected by the Kennedy family and a committee of architects to design the John F. Kennedy Memorial Library. I wrote stories about subjects who were interesting to me, whether they were male or female, famous or yet-acknowledged, young or old.

At times, my investigations and interviews took me on the road, and I had the opportunity to visit Chinatowns, cultural events, and conferences all over the country. Some of these trips revealed great stories, and others exposed a different kind of story, one that was still being told far too often in the lives of Chinese Americans. On one such occasion, I went to Lake Tahoe for a conference. I had made reservations for myself and for a cameraman who also worked for VOA. When we got to the hotel, the management refused to give me a room, saying they did not allow colored people in their establishment. I asked what they intended to do about the cameraman, but they did have a room for him. They snickered as I walked out of the hotel, carrying my suitcase (this was before suitcases had wheels), and set out on foot to try to find another accommodation. (I never wrote about that experience for the Voice of America.)

Chinese Activities found favor with listeners, especially with overseas Chinese communities in Southeast Asia, and I even began to receive fan mail. In addition to writing that program, I also wrote a weekly feature called *Americana,* which described some aspect of American life for the Chinese audience, and a weekly called *The Story Behind the Stamp,* which explained the origins of stamps issued by the US Postal Service. These scripts were far easier to write for than those for *Chinese Activities,* which posed a constant challenge to find new material firsthand.

There were some people at the time, including my husband, Bill, who felt that the Voice of America was little more than a vehicle for American propaganda overseas. Certainly, the news programming was written to give an American perspective on international matters, but the scripts I wrote about the lives of Chinese Americans were never designed to advance the cause of democracy in Asia. I wrote them to counter negative stereotypes and racism with positive stories and facts. In one script about the success of Chinese Americans in nearly every facet of life in Hawaii, I wrote, "Everywhere that the Chinese have migrated they have earned the respect of all by their hard work, their conscientiousness, and their levelheadedness." I wanted to share that reality with the wider world.

My job with the Voice of America rescued us from sure financial ruin and bought Bill more time to find a path that could work for him. He did not finish his degree but took a worldwide exam for calligraphers at the United Nations. When the results were reported, they hired him for $50 a week. Finally, we were both employed, and things were looking up.

❦ ❧

Chapter 6

LIVING IN AN ITALIAN NEIGHBORHOOD

In the 1950s, rentals were very scarce in New York. Few apartments had been built during the war because all available raw materials went toward the war effort. As veterans came back from World War II and began settling down, the market tightened further. Bill and I kept looking for a decent place to live, and eventually we found a housing project just beginning to go up in Bayside, Queens. That part of Bayside was barren land back then, with no utility lines or bus service extending that far from the city. The nearest grocery store was in the next town.

I remember that when we were finally able to move in, I had to take a big leap to go in and out of the apartment because the front stoop had not yet been poured. As we dragged our belongings up the walk to our new home and leaped over that stoop, a neighbor dashed out to greet us.

"I'm so glad this housing project will have a Chinese laundry," she gushed. "When will you be opening up?"

Even though the location of our new home was remote—which is hard to believe now—we finally had an apartment that felt like a home of our own. So many of the other Chinese students and young workers we knew did not have such a luxury. We entertained often, inviting other workers from the United Nations and students who were struggling to get by. In the privacy of our home, they were able to talk about news from China and the impact of Communism.

These conversations were far different from the ones I remembered from my childhood between my father and the other adults in our Washington community. At that time, "When are you going back to China?" or "Have you eaten?" were the standard greetings. As a girl, all those conversations about who was returning to China and when had left me with the impression that the country my parents had come from must be some sort of paradise.

But in the 1950s, things had changed. Returning to China was no longer an option for most people—and even if it had been, there was just debate about whether returning would be a wise or desirable choice.

CR&ED

Not long after our move, I discovered I was pregnant. The news was a shock to Bill. Instead of being happy, he was upset. He did not want a baby—he already felt trapped in a life that he had not desired or planned. Now that our lives were finally starting to take shape, he worried how we would survive if I had to give up my job and we had to live on his small salary.

Bill did not want me to have the baby, but even though I was frightened for our future, I refused to have an abortion. I wanted my child to be born.

I worked at Voice of America right up until the day before I went into the hospital to deliver. Bill became sick the same day—*sympathy sickness* was the 1950s diagnosis—and so he was hospitalized, too. I was on my own. I went to the hospital as my doctor had instructed me, only to find that all the maternity beds were full and I'd have to go to a different facility. I was scared to death during the entire, difficult birth. No one told me what was happening, but there was a terrible, hushed tension in the delivery room, and I knew something must be wrong. I gathered afterward from the nurses that the baby had been turned, her neck had been twisted, and the doctor had been concerned for us both. After 18 hours of labor, though, my little girl finally arrived. We named her Tina.

Bill was not happy to have a baby at all, and he would have preferred a son to a daughter. Though Tina was just an innocent, she seemed to represent all the things he could not control in his life: his stagnant career, his financial pressures, his unhappiness at losing his status in China, and finally, a rival for my time and attention.

I was in the hospital for six days of recovery, and for the entire time, Bill was in the other hospital with no diagnosis except sympathy pains. When the doctors finally said I could go home, it was Rose's husband, Arthur, who came to get Tina and me. He left us off at the apartment in Bayside. I was alone with my daughter for the first time. Even though I had taken care of children before, I knew nothing about caring for a newborn. I launched into the best routine I could figure out to keep a steady supply of bottles and formula and clean diapers available, and it seemed like I was washing or boiling or hanging something out to dry almost every minute I wasn't feeding Tina, who cried every three hours, day and night.

I'd expected to recover quickly from the delivery—after all, I had been perfectly healthy my entire life. Instead, I got more tired every day, and then after a few days at home, I felt a terrible pain in my lower abdomen. I called the doctor, but he assured me I was experiencing normal postpartum symptoms and told me to take an aspirin. I didn't even know what an aspirin was, let alone where I could get one or how I would manage to do so while I was in so much pain and alone with a baby.

When Bill finally came home, I collapsed in agony. He called for an ambulance and then called Rose, who came to get the baby and took her back to Hempstead, on Long Island. Rose had two young children of her own, and when she went to work, she left all three babies together with her caregiver. Tina would remain in childcare most of the time for many months while I was sick, Bill was working, and Rose and Arthur were running their busy restaurant.

At the hospital, a doctor examined me, diagnosed an infected gall bladder, and scheduled surgery for the next day. He did not order any blood tests but gave me a sedative to help me get through the night. The next day in the operating room, the surgeon quickly discovered there was nothing wrong with my gall bladder. He made a second incision and realized my appendix had ruptured, causing infection in my other organs. Thank goodness for antibiotics. Penicillin and streptomycin were both fairly new then, and the hospital pumped me full of both to save me. I received an antibiotic injection every two hours, day and night. I had to have a second surgery to try to clean out my abdomen, and during that operation the doctors had to remove an ovary and fallopian tube that had been ruined by infection. I had a lot of time in the hospital to think about the fact that I'd probably never be able to have another child.

The doctor who had been so neglectful on my admission was fired, and Bill had me moved to another hospital to try to get me better care. The night before I was scheduled to be discharged, the doctor on duty looked me over, noting that I was still very weak and ordered a transfusion. "She'll need it," he told the nurse. All through the night I was hooked up to a machine that dripped blood into my veins, but by morning, I was not feeling any stronger. I was delirious and ill. A nurse stopped the transfusion and put in an emergency call to the doctor who had ordered it. I'd been given the wrong blood type, and I was not going home anytime soon.

By the time I was finally discharged from the hospital, more than five months had passed, and I was still recovering from giving birth, a ruptured appendix, two surgeries, and an incompatible blood transfusion. I weighed just 89 pounds.

I went back to Bayside and saw my little girl for what felt like the first time.

With Tina, 1951.

I slowly regained my strength until I was able to go back to work. Until we could find a more suitable arrangement, Tina stayed during the week with the caregiver in Hempstead, where she was cared for alongside Rose's children, and Bill and I brought her home on the weekends.

Looking back, I realize I hardly knew her when she was a baby. We were just starting out together, and she was already five months old and away from home most of the time.

CR&O

Bill took the next level translators' exam with the United Nations, and he was one of the finalists. He was offered a promotion to a much higher professional status with a good salary. We decided to look for a house and found a well-built, brick two-family in the East Elmhurst area of Queens. Back then, East Elmhurst was a lively Italian neighborhood, and it was much closer to Manhattan, where Bill and I both worked, than our Bayside apartment. The house had three bedrooms, a living room, and a kitchen upstairs, with a garage and a small apartment downstairs. The rent downstairs would pay for the house, so we could live rent-free.

Almost everyone on our street was Italian except Bill, Tina, and me, and it seemed many of the families were somehow related to one another, though the exact ties were unclear to me. We were welcomed by everyone. I immediately liked the young lady who lived next door to us. She was outgoing and friendly and playful with Tina. Her name was Frances Galante, and before long she agreed to take care of Tina while I was at work each day, so I was finally able to bring my daughter home full time. Francie had a little boy of her own, and the two children got along wonderfully.

Francie lived with her husband and her parents, and Tina and I soon felt as if we'd been adopted into their family. The Galantes were wonderful to us. We were both invited to call the parents *Grandma* and *Grandpa*, and we gained a whole slew of other aunts, uncles, and cousins up and down our street.

No one locked their doors in East Elmhurst then. You could walk into any house in our neighborhood and you'd invariably be welcomed and invited to join a meal. I quickly learned the meaning of *mangia, mangia*. In hot weather, the neighbors brought stools outside, listened to someone play the guitar or accordion, sang songs, and even danced. As soon as she was big enough, Tina wanted to learn to play the accordion like some of our friends.

Tina and I loved our home and our neighborhood. Francie became a dear friend. I kept in touch with her for more than 60 years, until she died at age 92.

Unfortunately, Bill never became part of "our" Italian family. He was invited to join the men at different times, but he stayed inside and kept to himself. He was always worried about appearances. For the same reason, he was unwilling to help around the house in any way. He'd never dream of being seen carrying a baby or bringing home groceries or shoveling snow from the sidewalk.

"I am a scholar," is what he used to say if I asked him to help with something around the house. His beliefs were typical of a man born in China, especially one who had been singled out as one of the best and brightest of his generation and selected for the special privilege of a foreign education.

So I took care of the house and the baby and the sidewalk on my own before and after work. Despite the heavy workload, living next door to Francie and being a part of that lively community was a happy time for me.

છ ૭

Chapter 7

MORE CHILDREN, MORE ADVENTURES

With Bill's promotion, he became eligible for a paid home leave every two years. We applied to go to China, but it was off-limits to American citizens. We settled for visiting Hong Kong.

Bill, Tina, and I flew across the country and then boarded a ship to Honolulu, but when we arrived at the island, we were told the ship needed repairs that would take a day or two before we could continue. We were advised to take what we needed for a three-day stay and were put up at the Royal Hawaiian Hotel at Waikiki Beach. It was an opulent hotel right by Diamond Head Beach. Every morning, Tina and I went down by the water to dig in the white sand. We kept at it for hours. Tina was two years old then, but she was already showing signs of the personality she would develop. She was sociable and independent, happy to talk with anyone. She listened carefully and remembered much of what she heard. She was going to be a quick study.

While we were busy playing on the beach, the ship was hauled to a shipyard for a whole week. Other ladies at the hotel paraded through in their designer outfits—I even caught a glimpse of the tobacco heiress Doris Duke one day—but I just wore the two outfits I'd brought from the ship. Nevertheless, I enjoyed the beautiful surroundings.

We boarded the ship again, the unexpected gift of a luxury Hawaiian vacation over, and sailed across the Pacific to Yokohama, Japan.

At Yokohama, eight of us decided to visit Tokyo, an hour's train ride away. Our sightseeing group included a young Chinese couple, Bill and me, and four white Americans. Since the other Americans didn't speak Japanese or Chinese, they decided to tag along with us.

The Chinese couple's baby and Tina stayed on the ship with a child-care provider, and we all headed out together. The purser told us to be back on board by 3:00 p.m., when the ship would leave port for Manila.

We took the train to Tokyo, went on a tour, glimpsed the royal palace across a moat, had lunch at a Chinese restaurant, and then set out to go back to the ship. We decided to take two taxis to the train station. Bill and I split up. He took three of the Americans with him, and I took the Chinese couple and fourth American with me. Bill's taxi took off, but our driver, sensing we knew nothing about Tokyo, took off in the wrong direction, away from the station. I scribbled a note to the driver in Chinese saying we wanted to go to the train station, but he ignored me and kept going in the wrong direction. He would not respond to me. Finally, when he came to a stoplight,

I rolled down the window, flagged down a policeman, and wrote the characters for *train station* on a scrap of paper. The officer read it and ordered the driver to turn around and take us where we wanted to go.

When we finally got to the station, we were told we'd missed our train. The poor Chinese lady with me became hysterical. She stood there in the middle of the station, screaming and crying. Her baby was on the ship, and the ship was going to leave without us. Her husband tried to calm her down, and I scrambled to find any other way to get back in time. The ticket seller showed me a route we could take that might get us there with a transfer, and I grabbed my little group and boarded. As soon as we were all on, I went tearing from car to car, trying to find someone who spoke English to help us transfer. I met two Chinese American soldiers from Honolulu and latched onto them. One of the soldiers was actually the son of someone I'd interviewed for *Chinese Activities*, and he was happy to help us. The young men were not transferring at the same station as us, but they were gracious enough to put us on the right train for Yokohama before resuming their own journey.

When we got to Yokohama, the four of us jumped in a cab and told the driver to take us to the ship. The port was blocked by American sentries, but I didn't have time to explain. I just pulled the sentry into the cab with us. When we got to the dock, it was 3:10 p.m. and we saw our ship slowly moving down the dock. Passengers who saw us running started shouting for the ship to stop, and one man even shook the unsympathetic purser by his lapel. The longshoremen on the dock took a long board, put it through the garbage hole in the side of the ship, and told us to climb through.

We didn't argue. We just climbed up the plank as we were told. The young Chinese mother was so traumatized by the whole experience that she didn't leave her stateroom again until she got to Hong Kong.

Another traveler on that trip was a young man, a Chinese engineer who had been studying in America. Unlike Bill and most of his friends, who were open to the idea of Communism but not convinced it was going to be a great boon to China, this gentleman was avidly pro-Communist. Every chance he got, he would corner us and "preach" about how wonderful it was. He was determined to return, despite the travel challenges in and out, to become a part of Communist China's future.

After we arrived in Hong Kong, he took a boat to the mainland and offered the Chinese authorities his services. He was immediately taken into custody and stripped of everything he had, including the money he'd saved for his trip and his identification.

We saw him again in Hong Kong before we left, and he was not preaching the wonders of Communism anymore. Somehow he had managed to escape back to Hong Kong. He begged us to loan him some money so he could stay there.

CRBO

My own interest in spending time in Hong Kong was visiting my father. We intended to stay with him in Kowloon. After VJ Day was announced in 1945, he had gone back to China. His children were grown, and after toiling as a laundryman for 40 years, he felt it was time to go home. When he went back to our old house in Toishan, it was still standing, though the city around it was still in disrepair from the war. My father's nephew had been collecting rent from tenants in the house, but he had never paid the taxes. In arrears, my father sold that home and left to live in Hong Kong. He settled there and had bought property when the Communist reign began in China and homes in Hong Kong came into high demand.

I had not seen him in years, and I didn't know how we would take our reunion. He had remarried a nice widow who took good care of him. Father gave us the middle room in his apartment, which had no window and was stiflingly hot. We had a fan, but Bill complained about the heat until he finally went out and rented a room across the strait separating Kowloon from Hong Kong. The hotel did have air conditioning, but it was far away. We had to take a bus to a ferry, cross the strait, and then take another bus to the hotel. It was a disappointment to go all that way and spend so little time with my father.

CR&SO

Back in New York, we were settled and doing well in our jobs and in the Italian American neighborhood that had embraced us. I was elated, after all my days of worry when my ovary had been removed, to discover I was pregnant again. My son Victor was born on July 4, 1954. Everything was in place for him, and delivering him was quick and easy compared to the ordeal I'd gone through with Tina and the appendicitis that followed. I remember the nurses holding Victor up and admiring what a handsome baby he was.

Bill was happy to have a son, a male heir. When I returned to work, Victor was in the good hands of my friend Francie. She had also had another baby, and so my Tina and Victor and her Frankie and Annie became a foursome who spent their days together. When it was time for Tina and Frankie to start kindergarten a block from our house, they walked to and from school together. They were inseparable friends. My mind was completely at ease knowing my children were safe and loved while I was at work.

Right from the start, Victor was a curious and active boy. He would climb out of his crib and walk around in the night, and since we were upstairs, I went to great lengths to try to keep him contained. I put a guard on the stairs. I tried to escape-proof the crib. Finally, I consulted the pediatrician, who advised me to give the baby a teaspoon of red wine every night before bed. Somehow I don't think pediatricians are still giving that advice today, but it worked like a charm. After a couple months of quiet nights, I was able to dispense with the wine and Victor still slept through.

With Victor, 1955.

As he got older, Victor was quite a handful. I had to hook a leash to his pants when we took trips because he had a dangerous habit of disappearing. Some mothers would not dream of such a thing, but this child needed it to keep him safe. One night, on our next trip to Hong Kong, we were asleep on the ship when someone knocked at our cabin door at 2:00 in the morning.

There was the steward, holding Victor by the hand.

"Is this your little boy?" he asked. "He was found wandering the ship deck."

Victor was only a toddler, but he had climbed out of his crib and then out the porthole of our room! If our cabin had not been on the deck, he could have splashed into the ocean. After that, I kept a closer eye on him—and on the locks on doors and windows—for the remainder of the trip.

CʒꙄꙄ

When Victor was still very young, the Voice of America moved its headquarters to Washington, D.C. Rather than try to move my family or compromise Bill's job with the United Nations, I resigned. I had spent five years learning about Chinese ancestry, about the bravery and diligence of the earliest immigrants to America, and about the lives of Chinese American communities and families. Along the way, I'd improved my ability to speak Mandarin, honed my research skills, and learned to write a strong and engaging script. It was time to decide the next step in my career, but for a while, I would be more focused on family.

Two years after Victor was born, I delivered another healthy, eight-pound baby boy, and we named him Eric. When he was just a few weeks old, Eric developed a cough that kept him from sleeping, and so I took him to the pediatrician and was given a prescription for cough medicine. Back at home, I gave the baby half a teaspoon of the medicine after his bottle, and his whole body began to shake.

I called the pediatrician, and he told me to head straight to the hospital. At the emergency room, I filled out forms and related my family's medical history, but as Eric's shaking got worse, I lost my composure and screamed at the nurses to please take care of my baby. After my outburst, a nurse had me removed to another room, leaving the baby behind. She told Bill to take me home.

By the time we got back to our house, we had a message from the hospital telling us Eric had died.

I'll never know exactly what went wrong that day, but I was devastated at the loss of our baby boy.

I wanted to have another baby as soon as I could.

CRBO

In a little over a year, I was pregnant again, and Bill and I realized our family was outgrowing the little upstairs apartment of our Elmhurst house. I hated to leave our neighbors, but it was time. We bought a brick, split-level house on a dead-end street in Douglaston, a rustic, family-friendly neighborhood in Queens.

We were just settled in, in October of 1958, when Cynthia was born, a beautiful little girl with a full head of black hair. Two years later, in March of 1960, with two feet of snow in the forecast, I gave birth to my last and biggest baby, a boy we named Alan. After Alan was born, the snow just kept falling and falling outside, and most people in the city were stuck where they were when it started. At the hospital, patients and staff alike were snowed in, and relief personnel were snowed out. No new nurses came on at the end of each eight-hour shift, and so the ones who were there with us did what they could to maintain care. After 30 hours passed with no relief, the nurses were bone tired. Patients rang and rang their bells, but no one answered.

As soon as I was up and around, I did what I could to help. I gave out bedpans, helped care for mothers who had just given birth, translated for Chinese patients, and did whatever the nurses asked of me. For five days, the city was crippled by that storm, and no one came to see me until Bill arrived to take me home.

From then on, all the children were brought up in the Douglaston house. They all made friends in the neighborhood and then ran into and out of each other's homes as they played. We were a few blocks from the beach and pier where they could learn swimming and boating, and there was a huge patch of woods to explore just across the street. There was an excellent school three blocks away.

Every day in the summers, I'd open the front door and say, "Go," and they'd roam, scout, and explore the neighborhood. It was a great place to be a child.

In between taking care of the children and running our household, I worked part time in publishing. I worked for Channel Press, for a magazine called *Islands in the Sun*, and for Doubleday to help make ends meet.

Cynthia and Alan, 1964.

CR ಬಿ

Chapter 8

MOUNTAIN OF GOLD

Even though I was no longer working at Voice of America, the tales of Chinese immigrants to America and Chinese American families still occupied my thoughts, and the continuing perpetuation of negative stereotypes about both groups frustrated me to no end. I had written hundreds of scripts, full of historical and cultural facts that had been heard by a large audience on the other side of the globe, but they had never been broadcast in America—or even in the English language.

I did not set out to write a book, but the more I thought about it and researched the existing English-language literature, the more I thought there was a need for one, since no one had written from a Chinese American perspective. I felt I might be qualified to do the job, and so I started working on what would become *Mountain of Gold,* my first book. When Bill left for work and the children left for school, I set aside two hours to work on it each day. It took ten years because I depended on original research and interlibrary loans that sometimes came from esoteric places. When it was finally finished, I dedicated the book to my children, who shared and spared me so I could write a little while each day.

I gave my book the subtitle *The Story of the Chinese in America* and set out to chronicle the real history of Chinese immigration, settlement, persecution, and perseverance. Those first immigrants to America had risked everything—including a death sentence if they were caught—to try their luck at the Mountain of Gold.

As I continued to dig through library files, media clippings, and old census reports, I learned more than ever before about early Chinese immigrants and realized that most of them had come from Toishan or its vicinity—the same Chinese county my father had left to build his life in America. The Toishanese were historically pioneers and adventurers, and in the mid-1800s, they were the one Chinese population too tempted by the idea of prosperity in a new land to resist venturing out to see it for themselves. After the first immigrants gained a foothold in California, male family members followed, and the population of Toishanese in the American West exploded.

I wrote about Chinese men (and the early immigrants were almost all men) who were admired and in demand for their industriousness and strength and about how the governor of California had wanted to offer land grants to induce more Chinese to come. I wrote about how they were at first perceived as being weak and stupid by their hosts but then exceeded expectations at every task with which they were entrusted—from menial jobs like laundry and meal preparation to the manual labor of wresting gold from the earth, planting and harvesting fruit, and constructing the transcontinental railroad.

The book—and the history it was based on—had such a proud and hopeful start. But of course that was not the full story. What might have been a tale of acceptance and assimilation took a dark and ominous turn when the Chinese were targeted as scapegoats after the US economy fell on hard times. Chinese immigrants had become too successful in the eyes of some critics, and they were forced out of entire industries, and then, in the throes of a darkly racist anti-immigrant movement in the still sometimes-lawless West, many of them were persecuted for just being Chinese.

In 1870s San Francisco, a labor leader named Denis Kearney built a substantial following among working men and the press through his blatantly racist attacks on the Chinese. He was widely known for his thunderous and caustic speeches, many of which ended with his signature sign-off, "The Chinese must go!" Kearney's hate-filled rhetoric got him a great deal of attention not just in California but also in Boston and New York, and he played a key role in the eventual conception and legislation of the Chinese Exclusion Act of 1882. Kearney's period of popularity and fame kicked off a rash of violent attacks on Chinese workers. He was once even arrested for inciting a riot, but when the furor died down, the charges were dropped.

As I researched and wrote about slanderous campaigns, shocking attacks, and even murders, I kept focus on my goal of telling the story. Some of the details were almost too gruesome and cruel to comprehend, but my task was to make sure it was all documented. I wanted anyone who had an interest to be able to read the whole story.

Time and again, I ran into roadblocks in my research, and without the backing of Voice of America, I no longer had the luxury of visiting communities and libraries across the country to find what I needed. Thank goodness for interlibrary loans. I was one of the best "customers" at many libraries, and I could not have completed my research without the help of a number of knowledgeable librarians.

Throughout the process of creating the book, I wanted to write more like a storyteller rather than an academic, and so I filled my chapters with stories of real people and their experiences. I wrote about everyone from early settlers to my own peers, exploring the Chinese community's relationships with the American government, job market, religious institutions, educational establishment, and social structure. In many cases, the people I featured were characters from my own life, though I sometimes changed their names to protect their privacy or security.

One of the themes that emerged as the book took shape was the tumultuous relationship between Chinese and American immigration officials. I wrote about the passing of the Chinese Exclusion Act in 1882, the six-plus decades of blatantly exclusionary legislation that followed, and some of the abusive tactics that were employed by immigration officials as a result. I also delved into specific cases of Chinese businessmen, dignitaries, and students who'd been mistreated. One of the most illustrative examples of the unfair practices of immigration officials was the treatment of the Chinese delegates to the 1904 World's Fair in St. Louis. An American emissary had traveled to China to personally extend the government's invitation to this group, but the invitation was immediately followed with a list of insulting conditions. Each delegate must be photographed and subjected to identification through a system previously only used for criminals; each must submit a bond to be repaid upon his departure from the United States, and each was forbidden to leave the exposition grounds without written permission.

The list was an outrage.

Some of the most disturbing examples of the immigration system's failures and abuses were those of Chinese immigrants who were held in port-of-entry detention houses at the ironically-named Angel Island off the coast from San Francisco. This notoriously inhumane facility packed detainees into tiny, filthy spaces for weeks and even months at a stretch. Among them were many who became sick and even some who chose to take their own lives rather than face the shame of being sent back to China after having spent a life's savings— often not their own but a gift or loan from a family member—to get to America.

I explored the reasons why Chinese immigrants during the long decades of severe restrictions and outright omission were largely and notably law-abiding members of society, except with regard to what was considered the victimless crime of circumventing immigration law. This discussion of China's *paper sons* in America was not one my friends or neighbors wanted me to open, and I remembered well my father's reticence to even speak with the census taker. Still, I believed this was an important part of the history of the Chinese in America, and to leave it out would have been an irresponsible choice. I faced a disappointing backlash from my own Chinese community, which was adamantly against revealing the tactics that had once been used to evade immigration inspectors.

CR&CO

This particular issue was one that had directly touched my own family and my life. In 1961, Rose's husband, my brother-in-law Arthur Lem, endured a trial for being a paper son that was closely chronicled in the *New York Daily News* and Long Island's *Newsday*.

Arthur was 46 that year, and he had lived in the United States since he was 12. His was a classic story of a poor boy who became a self-made success. He'd gone from a high school kid working in a hand laundry nights and weekends to a successful restaurateur who was well known and respected in his town. He did volunteer work for the FBI and as a court interpreter, shepherded a drive that raised $25,000 for his local YMCA, and had been voted "Man of the Year" by his local business association. Arthur had always been a model citizen in his community—a hardworking business owner who employed many people and contributed to the local economy.

Yet, he was accused and tried for the "crime" of being a Chin, not a Lem.

During the trial, the speaker of the New York State Legislative Assembly, a college president, a deputy sent by former governor Thomas Dewey, and local judges all testified on Arthur's behalf, but the trial dragged on endlessly until he finally agreed to plead guilty to a single count of conspiracy to bring it to an end.

Even if Arthur Lem had a different name when he came to the United States as a young boy, was he really a criminal, deserving of public ridicule and sentencing? Had he even, at the age of 12, made that choice himself? I did not mention that Arthur was my brother-in-law in *Mountain of Gold,* but I could hardly exclude his story.

My book wound through the history of the Chinese in America, eventually coming to stories of success like those I'd written for Voice of America. These stories took on a new facet for me now that I had deepened my knowledge of the immigration struggles that preceded them.

As I worked on the book, I occasionally shared short stories and bits of information I was learning with my children, but for the most part, they were living a solidly American life in Queens, and they'd say things like, "Oh, Mom, why are you writing about old Chinese ways?" Only my young daughter Cynthia seemed to take much interest in my research, though the children were all proud of my work.

⚜

As *Mountain of Gold* took shape over nearly a decade, I finally began to think about getting a publisher. In those days, you had to send your book to one publishing house at a time for exclusive consideration, so it could be months or, more likely, years before it went under contract. In the 1960s, many publishers put out only about 150 books per year. I knew my book might never be selected into that very small group. I sent *Mountain of Gold* out to 15 publishers, one at a time. Most of the university presses responded that it wasn't academic enough, and while some of the trade publishers found the book interesting, they didn't feel there was enough of an audience to support it. One publisher after another sent the manuscript back to me, saying it was not right for them.

I still vividly remember the night I received a phone call from an editor at Macmillan who said *Mountain of Gold* was being accepted for publication. Tina and I danced around the living room, screaming with delight. I had labored on the book for so many years, and now it would be published and read. I felt incredibly honored that the publisher wanted it and even more so when the editor said almost no changes needed to be made to the manuscript.

Tina turned to Bill and asked, "Daddy, aren't you thrilled?"

His only answer was a grunt. He had never hidden the fact that he was not proud of my work, but this achievement made him resentful and sour. He wanted nothing to do with it.

CB&O

On Thanksgiving Day in 1964, my husband disappeared. Bill told me in the morning that he had to go to work, saying that the United Nations was not observing the American holiday. I spent the day with the children, preparing a Thanksgiving dinner. We waited and waited for him that night, but he had not gone to work. He had run off to Mexico to marry another woman.

My children were still very young—Tina, the oldest, was 14, and Alan, the youngest, was only four years old. I was shocked. Bill and I had been married for 16 years and had been through a lot together. I thought maybe he was just overwhelmed. I thought he was having a midlife crisis and that he'd come to his senses. I told him to come home to our family and we could forget the incident ever happened.

Bill had a shock of his own when he got to Mexico. He had mistakenly believed that since he was from China and an employee of the UN, he could have multiple spouses. The Mexican priest disagreed and refused to perform the wedding.

Bill did come home but not to reconcile. He came storming back and demanded that I give him a divorce so he could remarry. I tried to convince him to reconsider, but he said, "If you don't give me a divorce, I'll starve you to death."

I could not believe he would say such a thing, and I told him that if he starved me, he would starve his children, too. His response was that, yes, he would if he had to.

At that moment, the marriage was over for me. I could forgive him his coldness to me and his romp in Mexico with another woman, but I could not stay married to a man who'd threaten the well-being of his sons and daughters just to get his way. I signed the papers he'd brought, and he left.

I was in trouble, unemployed with a house to pay for and a family to feed. The agreement Bill had offered allotted me a small amount of alimony and child support, but after a few payments, he stopped paying. I hired a lawyer to go after the money, but the attorney fees ate up whatever I got. I asked the United Nations, Bill's employer, to garnish his salary, but they said they were not under the jurisdiction of any one country and did not have to obey US courts.

Bill was also supposed to take the children on weekends, but after a few weeks, he stopped showing up. He seldom saw them after that. It hurt the children to lose their father and to have him become so callous to them. Victor, especially, was at an age when he needed a father he could rely on, and he started getting in trouble at school and at home. I could hardly explain to the children what was going on in their father's mind that would make him choose a woman he hardly knew over his own family.

I knew I needed to raise them myself and make sure they felt they were still part of a strong and loving family.

A year later, Bill asked to come home, but we had moved on. I could not countenance him as a husband any more.

Through all the trials of this time, Rose was a rock for me. We are so different from one another—opposites in almost every way, but every time I have needed her in my life, she has stood ready to help me. I can't imagine what I would have done without her.

CℬꙄ

Everything about our day-to-day lives was more complicated once I became a single mother. I enrolled Alan in preschool day care because he was too young for kindergarten, and the older children had to fend for themselves after school. I couldn't afford to hire anyone to look after them.

At first, I took a job with *Colliers Encyclopedia* in the city, but being away all day and knowing the children were home and unsupervised left me angry and depressed. I quit that job and took a position at our local Queens Borough public library. Victor got a job shelving books there. Cynthia and Alan came to the library after school each day, did their homework and quiet reading there, and went home with me at 6 p.m. each evening. This was a better arrangement, and I was able to worry less.

Unfortunately, a clerical job at a library pays very little unless you have a degree in library science. I decided to go to Queens College at night to get one. It took a year and a half, but the children were all supportive, and Tina and Victor even took odd jobs to help with our expenses. Victor mowed lawns, delivered newspapers, and peeled onions for a delicatessen. We were a team with a goal, and I think working together through that hard time made us a closer family.

Once I had my library science masters, I was promoted to a better job with a higher salary at the library. Unfortunately, the branch manager job I'd hoped to achieve next went to a young man I trained and who got his degree after I did. The world was slowly changing in the 1960s, but men still had a heavy advantage in getting promotions.

CR ಬಿಂ

Chapter 9

FIRST ASIAN AMERICAN COURSES

T he publication of *Mountain of Gold* was more of a success than I could have dared to hope. In the media and in the academic world, it was received with kind and enthusiastic reviews. *Publishers Weekly* said it was "lively," "thoughtful," and "well-written." A professor of history from the State University of Washington said it was "absolutely delightful." The reviewer for *Twin Circle,* a Catholic digest based in California, said I had told the story of the Chinese experience with "breathtaking verve." John McAleer, a respected biographer and professor from Boston College, generously summed it up by saying:

> Although the Chinese constitute a bare one tenth of one percent of our population, their rights are the same rights enjoyed by other citizens. Yet by tradition they are so schooled in courtesy and so ashamed at loss of face they accept humiliations without protest. As a result, the extent to which they have been deprived of their rights—though their

contribution to American life has been much beyond their numbers—is dismal to consider. Till now it has scarcely been considered at all.

Dr. McAleer went on to say that any American who had a humane interest in civil rights had an obligation to read the book.

Senator Hiram Fong from Hawaii gave me a great honor when he read a summary and review of the book to the US Senate on December 8, 1967 and his speech became part of the permanent *Congressional Record*. His speech, in part, said, "I am delighted and pleased to call the attention of senators to this very excellent book and to commend it without qualification to all persons who may be interested in the story of one of America's minority groups."

Both the publisher and I were thrilled with the reviews.

Sales were brisk, in part because the recognition the book received from the academic world. The Chinese community also fervently embraced the book. It was adopted by several institutions of higher learning for use in academic courses.

In my personal life, I was suddenly treated with a new regard that was a wonderful validation. My doctor told me he'd stayed up all night reading *Mountain of Gold* and overslept the next morning for his hospital rounds. I overheard two brothers discussing the book in Florida and shocked them by telling them I was the author. Even years and decades later, people would sometimes hear my name and pause, putting things together, and then ask if I was the author of *Mountain of Gold*. I even met a lady from South America on a cruise who told me she loved it.

The publication of *Mountain of Gold* opened up a new career path for me. I received an invitation from City College of New York to teach the first full-time college course in Asian American culture and history. At the time, the school was one of the oldest colleges in the nation and had a very selective enrollment process, but tuition was free. For both of these reasons, City College had earned a reputation and nickname as the poor man's Harvard. In its long history, though, the college had always been dominated by white males—no women and few blacks or other minorities—even though the campus was situated in Harlem.

That was all about to change. In the spring of 1969, an organized group of hundreds of students padlocked the gates to the college's south campus and took over a number of buildings, effectively shutting down the college until their demands were met. They wanted the college to accept more minority students. As was often the case in the late 1960s, protest was an effective way to create change.

What rolled out in the years that followed this standoff was a radically different admissions program from the one that had existed since the 1800s.

In a matter of just a few years, by 1972, CCNY went from being an exclusive program primarily for white men to the largest degree-granting institution for minorities in the country. City College and City University of New York, together consisting of more than 20 colleges, switched from an exceedingly selective application process to an open admission policy. Open admission meant that anyone with a high school diploma could get into City University.

In the first year alone, enrollment doubled, and the demographics and academic qualifications of the student body changed dramatically. The students became much more racially diverse, meeting the key goal of the policy change. The student body also became much more academically diverse as a result of open admissions, and many of the incoming students after this policy went into effect had lower grades and test scores than the college had been accustomed to in its students.

As a result, every member of the faculty was required to teach a remedial math or remedial English course. In addition to trying to forge an Asian American studies program where none had previously existed during those early years of my teaching career, I also taught one of those English courses. As someone who had never felt confident of my ability in the fundamentals of the language, I can honestly say that teaching remedial English was one of the most difficult tasks I've ever had to undertake.

CB&O

It was 1970 when I started at the college, and there was almost nothing in the school's libraries for my students to read that was relevant to my classes. As I constructed my curriculum, I was very mindful of the single Asian studies course I had taken during my own college years—a recitation of the encyclopedia on the subject—and I was determined to create relevant, instructive courses that offered my students depth and insight. As a result, nearly everything we used in my classes was from primary or empirical sources. I fashioned my courses by digging into the Chinese communities firsthand. I immersed myself in Chinese American activities not just as a participant but as a teacher looking for ways to impart understanding to my students.

I taught about some of the material I'd covered in *Mountain of Gold*, including the history of Chinese immigration to America and the hardships and accomplishments of those immigrants over time.

I taught about the challenges to assimilation and about the insular institutions Chinese immigrants had initially created to help make sure the basic needs of their peers were met.

In addition to teaching my students about history, I wanted them to learn about the present. I often required students to do work in the community as a part of their educational experience. I worked with contacts at social service agencies like the immigration service, the Chinatown Planning Council, and the Organization of Chinese Americans to place my students in volunteer positions where they could help immigrants who did not yet speak English or understand American culture. When one of these organizations needed volunteers, I sometimes offered an extra course so my students could earn college credit by providing assistance in the Chinese American community.

There was a great need for social services during this time because it was a period of a huge influx of Chinese immigrants. American immigrations laws had undergone a dramatic shift following the Immigration and Naturalization Act in 1965. Before that, all Asians had been barred from the United States by the 1924 Act, which named them as "aliens ineligible to citizenship." During World War II, when the United States was fighting Japan, the Chinese Exclusion Act of 1882 had been repealed, but only 105 Chinese citizens were allowed to enter the country each year. That number jumped to 20,000 Chinese citizens with the 1965 law. Because many people continued to flee Communist China for better lives elsewhere, some of these immigrants arrived in the United States through refugee acts as well.

These changes were reflected in a major shift in the motivations for immigration from those of the past; many of the Chinese of this time were not coming to America primarily to seek their fortunes but rather to escape their misfortunes. Many arrived penniless and ill equipped to adjust to life in America. They desperately needed the support of state and local agencies to find their footing.

CℬℬↃ

College students in those days had a very strong voice in institutions of higher learning. In keeping with the no-holds-barred politics of the civil rights movement that just preceded their time, they demanded to be heard, sometimes through methods that could be construed as disrespectful or even aggressive. They blocked entrances, commandeered offices, marched, and rallied to grab and hold the attention of the administration.

Many students of this time felt that the courses they were taking had no relevance to their own lives, and they wanted to change that. Some felt an overwhelming desire to express themselves about the Vietnam War and the issues it brought to mind—including compulsory military service, wars of aggression, Communism, the scope and limits of America's responsibility and authority in the world, and what role the government could and should play in their lives. The draft was still in effect at this time, and it was not uncommon for me to encounter students who were enrolled in my courses, in part, to defer their military service.

I first discovered this when one very bright young man wanted to drop out of my course in the middle of the semester. I was puzzled because he was doing so well and seemed fully engaged in the class, but close inquiry revealed that he simply did not want to finish school. If he finished his degree, he would have to go to Vietnam, and that was the last thing in the world he wanted to do.

In general, my students were strongly opposed to the war and were outspoken about it. Many were also actively involved in the community in ways that extended far past the participation I required of them. They spent extra hours helping out in agencies that assisted newly arrived immigrants. They volunteered in local schools and community groups. They advocated for some of the poorest and most ignored members of New York's population. Even today, many of those men and women are still active leaders and helpers in the community. Some of my former students have even retired from long and lucrative careers and then taken on larger roles of service to New York's Chinese American population.

Another issue my students found worthy of their protests was the grouping of black studies, Puerto Rican studies, and Asian American studies courses under the single blanket title of Department of Ethnic Studies. The students wanted separate departments and a wider variety of course offerings. They wanted more courses that were relevant to the community. At different times in the early 1970s, students from each ethnic group and their supporters staged protests and other events on campus to make this point. In 1972, a group of students of Asian descent took over Goethals Halls at CCNY to force a change. Over the days that followed, over 300 protesters joined them, including black and Puerto Rican CCNY students, Asian American students from other local campuses, and community groups. The protesters shut down the college, halting all classes until their demands were met.

As a result, the small offering of Asian American studies courses that existed became an Asian Studies Department incorporating courses in East Asian history and culture. The creation of this new academic department produced a need for courses that explored a range of Asian countries and regions. The college also began offering Asian language courses, including Cantonese, Mandarin, Japanese, and Hindi. This was a huge victory for the students because Asia and Asian languages had never been previously acknowledged in the curricula.

With these changes, the Asian Studies Department expanded to include Dr. T.K. Tong, a well-known Chinese historian, and Dr. Diana Kao, who taught both the Cantonese and Mandarin classes. Adjunct faculty taught other courses, and I began to expand my own base of knowledge beyond the history of Chinese immigration in America to include a wider history and background of other Asian groups. Peoples from more than a dozen separate national and regional groups were represented by this new department, and students from all of them wanted courses that included their backgrounds.

In addition to the courses on the Chinese and Chinese Americans I'd been teaching all along, I began teaching a course about Asian American women that delved into the traditional roles women occupied in a number of cultures and how those roles changed in America. I was interested to learn that the submissiveness that was so valued in traditional Chinese and Japanese society did not universally translate to other Asian cultures. Some, like the Malaysians, looked to women as the matriarchs of their families.

I also taught courses in Asian American relations. I had to research and learn about the cultures of many groups, including the Japanese, the Koreans, the Vietnamese, the Filipinos, the Malaysians, and the Indians. In my classes, I sometimes assigned students to form groups by ethnicity, research their own immigration story, and report it to the class. I ran into trouble with this procedure one year when I asked two Indian students to work together and speak to the group. One of these young men blurted out that he could not speak to the other, because they were of different castes.

I stopped the class then and there, and we talked about the caste system. In the end, though, I let the two students give their talks separately rather than force them to work together.

CRITSRIO

I began my career at City College with a bachelor's degree from the University of Illinois and a master's in library science from Queens College, but despite my lack of a higher degree, I quickly advanced to assistant professor and then associate professor and obtained tenure. Apparently, someone thought I had potential in the administration, and I was selected as one of three fellows to train under the chancellor in charge of all 20-plus colleges in the university system. One of my tasks in this role was to identify candidates for promotion. I was given instructions to eliminate anyone without a doctorate from the roster for upward movement. I was flabbergasted. I did not have a doctoral degree.

As it turned out, my appointment despite this shortcoming had been an oversight. As soon as the powers that be discovered I did not have a Ph.D., I was demoted. I even had to pay back the monies I'd received as an associate professor.

I decided then that I would earn a Ph.D.

Chapter 10

A NEW FAMILY

Charles Chia Mou Chung had been a friend and colleague of my former husband, Bill. Charles was born in China and had gone to the police college in Chungking before becoming one of the first people selected by the Chinese government to come to the United States for higher learning. He was enrolled at New York University for his doctorate when Mao Tse-Tung took over China, and that change in the politics of his country changed the course of his life. After struggling to get by without any support from home, Charles found work at the United Nations.

People were drawn to Charles because of his amiable personality, and wherever he went he found a new friend. As a UN reviser who edited other people's translations, Charles's written English was excellent, but his pronunciation was awful. This, like his unassuming manner and trusting nature, was part of his charm. In addition to his job with the UN, Charles traveled extensively to buy and sell jade, Oriental art, and jewelry.

It was not easy for a Chinese man in America to find a suitable wife at that time, so Charles had married late in life. Like many traditional Chinese men, he'd wanted a son to carry on his family name. His first three children were girls, and the fourth a boy. His family was complete, but while their son was still very young, Charles's wife had divorced him and left him with the children.

Charles began calling me, and we got along so easily that pretty soon we were in the habit of talking on the phone every night from 11 until midnight. It was a late hour, but we both had full schedules and busy family lives. That time after the children went to bed became the time we shared with one another.

Decades later, on the occasion of my 80th birthday, Charles wrote a beautiful letter about our relationship for inclusion in a book to celebrate the day. He wrote "After my repeated proposals to marry me, Betty finally agreed . . . We got engaged, and married on July 22, 1972. That was 32 years ago and was my very luckiest day."

Charles did propose many times. For two years, we had been friends, but I was not ready to get married again. In the end, it was more than Charles's proposals that convinced me to marry him—it was also the time I spent with his children. Charles's four children were all still young then, the littlest just a preschooler. Without a mother at home, their lives had been full of turmoil. Charles had to go to work, so his daughters were often left at home, staring at the television all day. His son Calvin, only three years old, was in the care of another family. Anyone could see the children were having a hard time. When Charles brought his four children to my house, they got along easily with my children.

I knew before I married him that Charles would never help around the house. In Chinese culture, a scholar never dirties his hands, and if there was one thing I'd learned in my years of study up to then, it was that it's hard to change cultural habits. I knew that he would still travel every other weekend for his business and that I would be left behind with all the children.

I consulted with Rose, and even though she thought taking care of four more children would be a challenge for me, she believed that Charles was a good man.

Charles and I were married in New York in 1972 with all the children present, and afterward, we celebrated at a restaurant on Park Avenue. Rose was there to celebrate with us. After the wedding, Charles and his children moved into my house in Douglaston. I don't remember the move being much of a fuss—even though our two small families were combining to one big one. The children already knew one another. We shuffled the bedrooms a bit—Cynthia shared her bedroom with Vivian, Alan with Calvin, and Charles and I took the master bedroom. Then everyone got on with their lives. Victor stayed at college at Cornell. Charles's two oldest daughters attended

Marriage to
Chia-Mou Chung, 1972.

the United Nations school, so they stayed at Charles's apartment near Chinatown with Tina, who had graduated from Princeton and was working in Manhattan. She looked out for her stepsisters, and all the girls came home to join us on weekends and holidays.

In the summer, when I wasn't teaching, we went out to Fire Island to visit Rose, her husband Arthur, and her boys. Milton's children would join us, and we would go clamming, foraging for mussels, fishing, and swimming. Arthur was an accomplished fisherman, and when he headed down to the dock in the morning, he'd ask what kind of fish we wanted for dinner—and he'd often bring it back. The cousins played together in the sand and the water, and everyone had a happy time.

CR&O

Back in the Douglaston house, after a period of adjustment Charles's withdrawn little boy started to come out of his shell. He looked up to Victor and Alan, and they loved having a little brother. They took him with them sometimes when they went out, drilled him on his multiplication tables, and got him involved in Cub Scouts. By that time, Alan was well on his way to being an Eagle Scout. Every evening, all the children did their homework together at the dining room table, and when one of them struggled with a subject or assignment, the others pitched in and helped.

Charles and I were delighted to see how quickly we all began to feel like part of one family.

Mountain of Gold had been published two years before, but instead of being intimidated by my success, Charles was always proud of my work and my professional accomplishments. He loved to introduce me to his friends and tell them about my books and my teaching. He was a very active community leader in his own right. He was president of his college alumni association, the Hakka Association, and a member of the Chinese Consolidated Benevolent Association in New York. We were both well known in the Chinese community of New York. We disagreed about many things—politics and cultural traditions among them—but it didn't matter. We were happy and secure in our marriage.

Juggling a family of ten, a demanding teaching career, and the pressures to do original research and earn my Ph.D. was a tremendous challenge. Thankfully, the children were a huge help. I'd give them a list of chores—including laundry and ironing, packing lunches, keeping their rooms clean, and helping with dinner preparations— and they'd all pitch in to make our family life work. When the house needed repainting, all the children got involved, and we finished the job lickety-split. Alan especially had a knack for fixing things even though he was just a little boy. Whenever I needed any plumbing, electrical, or other handyman's job, he usually was able to figure how to do the repair.

The children rotated their duties so that everyone had each of the household jobs in turn. If one child reneged on his efforts, we all suffered and we let that person know it, so it didn't happen very often. I made lists for breakfast, lunch, and dinner and shopped for food twice a week—usually in huge quantities. I generally cooked the dinner, but the children did most of the prep work.

Dinner was at seven, and we all sat down to eat together every night. That's when we related our days and told each other our stories and jokes. This was family time, and I insisted that we all be present. I also insisted that everyone spoke, even if just a single sentence. At first, Charles's children were not accustomed to speaking up, and they would respond with a single syllable while we waited for a full sentence. But after a while, it was difficult to keep them quiet. Everyone had plenty to say, and our dinner table was always a bois-terous one.

At the end of the day, after the children had gone to bed or their separate ways, I'd spend an hour or two working on my degree or my writing. All children have distinct memories that stay with them, but one memory that mine all seem to share is falling asleep to the sound of my typewriter click-clacking away from my room upstairs.

CR EO

Chapter 11

CHINA UNDER COMMUNIST RULE IN 1973

The Bamboo Curtain fell over China shortly after Mao Tse-Tung took the reins of government in 1949. His rule was almost airtight. No one was allowed to leave China, and few were allowed to enter. The airwaves were monitored and jammed, and any violations were dealt with swiftly and severely. The United States was declared China's number one enemy and a paper tiger.

In 1972, after almost a quarter century of China's mainland being shut off from contact with other nations, President Nixon and Secretary of State Henry Kissinger reestablished relations between the two great countries. China began to open its borders to US citizens. Since Charles was with the United Nations and had not visited his home country in decades, we applied to visit.

We filled out pages and pages of information about ourselves, waited for the Chinese bureaucracy to approve us, and then waited interminably for our visas. They finally came in the summer of 1973.

Everyone was approved except Tina, who was considered an adult and no longer eligible for UN home-leave subsidy. That left seven children accompanying us. We had to get vaccinated for diphtheria, typhoid, and yellow fever, registering all the shots and then carrying the record with our passports in a little yellow booklet.

Once we received the coveted visas, we planned the trip with great excitement. We made our itineraries to cover some separate ground, because I wanted to go to Toishan, and Charles wanted to combine his trip with buying art objects in China and visiting his hometown.

China was so secretive that no one knew what was going on behind the Bamboo Curtain. I returned there, wanting to see what was going on and hoping to do something to help the extended family members I had not seen for so many years. When we landed in Hong Kong, I went straight to the government stores that knew what was scarce and needed on the mainland and what was allowed into China. It was ironic that bicycles made in China were shipped to Hong Kong and then reshipped back to China—you couldn't just buy the bicycle in China. A bicycle was a highly prized possession, as it was the only means of transportation available to most people and almost a necessity in farming. I bought four bicycles, two sewing machines, six rolls of cloth (only black, blue, and grey were allowed), gallons of cooking oil, pounds of tea and sugar, and several made-in-Shanghai watches.

I had to pay to have everything crated by a carpenter to ship to *Lo Wu* and then to Canton. Once we crossed the border, everything had to be unboxed and inspected, and we had to submit to an hours-long examination with customs officials. We would be escorted, followed, and watched for the entirety of our visit, but we were finally allowed onto the train to Canton.

The euphoria of entering China was still there, but my immediate impression was that we were in a different world. We stood out with our many children, our colorful Western clothes, and our freedom to spend money and travel. We were nonconformist in a land of complete conformity, and I even heard people calling us "ugly" for our differences.

I had lived in Toishan from 1934 to 1938. Charles had grown up in China and did not leave until he was 26, but this society was different. It was intensely organized and rigid. Compliance was expected from every person in every situation.

It was also very clean. There were cleaners everywhere. One person was assigned to keep our train car spotless. She cleaned the one car from one end to the other and back again all through the day. The train ran on coal, and the smoke from the engine covered us all with soot and ash, but nevertheless, our train car was immaculate. Things were the same way in the streets. One person was assigned to one block, and he or she swept the street and kept it clean. No one dared throw trash on the streets.

挃挃

During our entire trip in China, we were accompanied by government officials who explained the policy and rules and ensured that we did not overstep our bounds. At each city, we were assigned a person who stayed with us the entire time and even slept next door to us at the hotels. How strange it seemed that it was someone's job to watch over us—not for our protection, as far as we could tell, but to make sure that we did not contaminate others with our ideas.

When we checked into the Overseas Chinese Hotel, no one offered to help us with the luggage. I asked for a bellboy but was told that there was no such position, and that everyone was equal. In other words: *Carry your own luggage.* It was not the first or the last time I felt distinctly American in the country where my parents were born and where I spent years of my childhood, and it would not be the last.

We were given quarters on the seventh floor. The seventh and eighth were reserved for visitors from the United States and Canada. The third and fourth floors were for guests from Southeast Asia, and I learned later that the beds on those floors were lined up like a ward in a hospital—one big room for everyone. You were assigned a bed, not a room, and you slept with your belongings beneath it because there was no room for them anywhere else.

The hotel had separate accommodations for each group based on their country of origin and status, and it did what it could to prevent intermingling among the guests.

Meals at the Overseas Chinese Hotel, and for that matter everywhere, were very rigidly scheduled, with breakfast at eight, lunch at noon, and dinner at six. Ration tickets were required for meals, and if you had no ticket, you received no food. One night when the children and I were ready to go to dinner, Charles wanted to take a nap and told us to go ahead without him. When he got up and was ready to eat, the kitchen said it was too late to serve him. He went outside the hotel and found a restaurant, but the place would close at eight and the chef could not work overtime. In fact, everything would close at eight. Everyone worked for the government in one capacity or another, and everyone kept the same hours: eight to noon, then a siesta from noon to three, then three to eight in the evening. Overnight and between the hours of noon and three, the country was effectively shut down. That night, Charles finally gave up on finding supper and tried to buy bread from a street vendor. Even here, he was unsuccessful. He could not find his ration tickets. The vendor would not take money and took the bread back from Charles. In the end, he just went hungry.

Every morning during this part of our stay, Charles's family arrived, including his father, his mother, his grown nephew, and his little nephews. They lived in the Kowloon Territories but spent their days camping out in our hotel rooms. They were not allowed to eat in the Overseas Chinese Hotel.

Charles's father was typically, overwhelmingly chauvinistic. When he came to the hotel, he took off his shoes, sat on the bed, and expected everyone to wait on him. Charles's mother was a delight. She was in her late 70s or early 80s, but she managed all the children and grandchildren with ease. When she took us to the train station, she picked up our two suitcases, pushed ahead of the crowd, got on the train, and reserved seats for all of us.

She was accustomed to doing all the work, and if she resented it she did not give it away. I thought back to my childhood, to all the hours I'd spent angry about having to wait on my brothers. I remembered the hard resolve I'd had to find to defy my father and go to college. I had been born to be a submissive and dogged worker, too, but even as a child I'd been unable to abide it.

During our trip, we had the opportunity to do some amazing sightseeing. In Beijing, we visited the newly opened Forbidden City, where the emperors of China had once lived. We saw the throne on which the emperors sat and the priceless treasures in the palaces.

Then we boarded a bus to the Great Wall, one of the eight wonders of the world. I had never seen it before. It is miles north of Beijing, and at that time it took hours to get there. The Wall was built more than 4,000 years ago and stretches across northern China from east to west. How it was built without modern machinery remains a mystery to this day.

When we visited, the Wall was in advanced stages of disrepair. Only one steep section up to the first guardhouse was open to the public. I climbed slowly to the guardhouse, but coming down was extremely difficult. I remember finally lying down and sliding. I simply could not walk it.

Everywhere we traveled, the presence of Mao Tse-Tung and the government was ubiquitous. In Beijing, several times a day the radio would come on automatically, and government decrees would be announced. Mao had decreed that the entire nation use the Mandarin dialect, and so everywhere you turned, there were signs that said, "Speak Mandarin."

I wanted to talk with everyone I met, to find out how they were doing and what life in China was really like, but my behavior made the government officials suspicious of me. They seemed to think I was a spy and even took away my camera.

The China of 1973 was nothing like the China I remembered from my childhood. There were so many rules and rigid strictures, and people were separated by origin, sex, class, and race. Yet everyone was supposed to be equal. I remember going to a doctor while we were there, and it only cost ten cents (in Chinese money). She opened a drawer and took out a tongue depressor and placed it in my mouth, then she wiped it off and put it back to use again on the next patient.

It was the only one she had. I thought that if I had not already been ill, I surely would be the next day.

The doctor gave me a black medicine in a bowl and told me to take it, but I decided not to. I didn't know what to think. In the old days, if you got sick and didn't have any money, you died. Under the Mao regime, we were sharing tongue depressors and receiving mysterious medications, but anyone could go to a minimally trained "barefoot doctor." It cost next to nothing.

I, for one, could not decide which was the better system.

CRe80

Upon arrival in Canton, I had applied for a bus ticket to Toishan. Then I waited. Each day, I was denied. On the third day, I decided to go to the bus station and buy the tickets myself. The China Travel Service tried to dissuade me, but I was determined to go to Toishan, the county from which the earliest Chinese emigrated and my childhood home. At the bus station, five different tellers said there were no tickets available.

"You can't go," one of them told me.

I lost my temper and finally shouted that even if I had to stand all the way, I was *going*. I guess no one had questioned their control over the bus tickets before, because the tellers hurriedly assembled in a back room. After much discussion, they came up with two tickets for the next day's bus. Cynthia, who continued to share my interest in China and its history, was coming with me, and we'd soon be on our way.

Questioning had revealed that three buses left daily, all at 6:20 a.m. The distance was about a hundred miles, but it would take approximately five hours to make the trip because we had to cross three rivers, and the ferries would not move unless there were enough vehicles aboard. When we boarded the bus in the morning, we discovered that what looked like a two-seat bench was intended for three people. The bus was packed full, not just with people but with squawking chickens and squealing pigs as well.

The best part of the ride was when we got off the bus and sat on the riverbank to wait for the ferry to fill up. Everyone was talking and laughing, and soon they were asking me questions about the United States. I was surprised, because the Mao government had painted the United States as China's enemy for its support of Taiwan and for preventing Communist China's representation in the United Nations. Yet among the travelers on the bus with us, the underlying feeling for the United States was warm and friendly.

We arrived at 12:30 p.m. and were met by the county mayor and a large delegation that treated us to lunch. When I said I'd like to hire a car to take us to my village, I was met with blank stares. There were no automobiles in that county. We could either ride on a wheelbarrow or take a rickshaw. We opted for the latter.

My cousin, the son of my father's brother, and his wife were the only relatives of mine left in the village. The whole area had been devastated during the Japanese occupation and in many ways had not fully recovered. My cousin lived in the same house my father built, but it had fallen into disrepair. I gave them the gifts I had brought. My brothers and sister had each contributed $50 to my gift fund, so I had brought $200 worth of presents for my cousin and his wife. That was a huge sum then because the exchange rate was seven

Reminbi to one US dollar, and the average pay for a laborer was ten *Reminbi* a month.

At one time, Toishan had been a showcase county because the overseas Chinese loved their hometown and contributed to its modernization and facilities. When I lived there as a child, there was a gleaming white building that housed the county government offices, and right next to it was a public library, but now the buildings were shabby and war worn. Toishan had boasted a railroad that ran all the way from Canton because the Chinese men who built the Transcontinental Railroad in America wanted their home county to have a railroad, too. Sadly, the tracks from Toishan were torn up during the Sino-Japanese war to use their iron for weapons, and the railroad has never been restored.

Cynthia and I made our way back to the Overseas Chinese Hotel the same way we'd come—by a rickshaw and ferries and a bus loaded down three-to-a-seat with squawking chickens and squealing pigs in between.

When we packed up and left the country, our entire family was examined again. We were told that nothing could leave China that did not come into the country with us, not even the newspapers we had wrapped our shoes in.

CR ƏD

Chapter 12

DIFFERENTIATING THE CHINESE FROM "OTHERS"

Teaching in an institution of higher learning meant expanding the field of knowledge. After Charles and I returned from our first trip together to China, I turned my attention to research and publication.

It was my students who made me consider how little statistical information was available about the Chinese in America. I was often asked to provide answers to questions for which no information existed, things like, "How many Asians are there in Washington?" "What is the birth rate in the Chinese community in New York City?" or "What percentage of the Chinese community works in restaurants?"

The Manpower Administration of the Department of Labor was also asking questions and was particularly interested in how new Chinese immigrants were fitting into the US economy. Neither the Census Bureau nor the Department of Vital Statistics seemed able to provide any answers. The US census, taken every ten years, asked the question of race, but not until the 1980 edition would those answers be broken down by ethnicity. Before then, the Chinese were lumped into the category of "Other." Determining the circumstances of the Chinese seemed impossible.

A great deal of unanalyzed information existed that could be examined to gather this information, so I applied for a grant from the Manpower Administration, whose particular interest was Chinese American employment characteristics. When I received the grant, I headed to the Lawrence Radiation Lab at the University of California at Berkeley to delve into who the people who checked "Chinese" and were statistically counted as *"Others"* were and how they might be scrutinized with an eye toward shedding light on the employment patterns of America's foreign- and native-born Chinese. My daughter Cynthia was still in high school at the time, but she came with me during the summer and became an invaluable companion, assistant, and typist.

To begin, I took the census questionnaires from 1970 and culled out anyone who had written "Chinese" on the form. With this information flagged, the census lab was then able to identify the Chinese through all the other filters of their database, including state, county, city, age, sex, and many social and economic factors. This information was published by Arno Press of the *New York Times* and established the first database of Chinese Americans.

Prior to the next census, I served on the Census Advisory Committee, and all of us in that group recognized the importance of breaking down the race category into separate ethnicities so that this kind of work would not have to be done again in the future.

CB&O

Since I was already delving deeply into the census, I decided to kill two birds with one stone. The same grant that allowed me to separate out the census responses also provided support for me to create a snapshot of the economic characteristics and occupational status of Chinese Americans, and so I continued to use the 1970 census to ascertain the kinds of employment in which the Chinese were engaged. The biggest drawback to this approach was that even in 1975, the census data was already out of date. Since the Immigration and Naturalization Act of 1965, Chinese men, women, and children had been flocking to the United States. At the time I published my findings, approximately one-fourth of the Chinese population in America had arrived *after* the 1970 census.

I also knew at the outset of my study that the actual numbers of Chinese in America would be underrepresented. When I was a child, my father had mistrusted the census taker who knocked on our door. There were undoubtedly still countless individuals who felt the same way—people who would avoid giving complete and accurate information to the census taker because they perceived maintaining their anonymity as a means of protecting themselves and their families. After eight decades of forced exclusion and radically restricted legal immigration, the ghosts of illegal and extralegal entry still haunted the Chinese in America, and many opted to avoid government officials whenever possible.

Years later, in 1981, I conducted a census undercount review for the Census Bureau. The undercount, using a sample street in Chinatown for reference, was indeed a large percentage of all eligible participants.

I knew it was likely the Chinese respondents who did fill out their questionnaires would be skewed toward native-born, better-educated, English-speaking individuals, many of whom lived beyond the bounds of Chinatowns. I had to acknowledge from the beginning that this group would be better represented in my sample than their foreign-born peers, many of whom spent their entire lives in America within the bounds of insular ethnic communities.

Unfortunately, it was those who did not respond who might have most benefited from an accurate accounting, since one of the objectives of my work was to find ways the government could help foster assimilation in the labor market.

I tried to test and corroborate my findings about where people were living, what jobs they were doing, and how well they were paid by talking to Chinese people young and old, foreign born and native born, from all walks of life, and from different regions of the country. I studied the listings at employment offices in the Chinatowns of San Francisco and New York. I interviewed men and women in their fields. I had long talks with my graduating seniors to find out how they went about applying for jobs and how they felt about their prospects for finding work. My research assistants worked to ascertain the pay scales for each occupation.

As I worked on the study, I became increasingly persuaded that occupation may be the single most important aspect of any adult life. It takes up the largest portion of our waking hours and provides the means for our existence. It determines where we live and how we live. It may circumscribe our social life. It seemed to me that many Americans considered choice of occupation as a basic right and had perhaps given little thought to the fact that even in the United States, career choice is restricted by many factors—including citizenship, language facility, and ethnic background. These limitations can even carry over from one generation to the next. Time and again I heard stories of American-born children of Chinese parents who felt they were as red, white, and blue as the next kid—only to be reminded by an admissions officer or a hiring manager that their physical features nevertheless caused them to be treated like foreigners.

I came to believe that understanding the occupational status of any group is fundamental to understanding them. After all, if one segment of the population has always been slaves, CEOs, laundrymen, or farmers, that experience helps inform the way those people see the world and their place in it.

As I spent my days poring over census samples at the Lawrence Radiation Lab at Berkeley, some patterns began to emerge—a few that I had anticipated and others that were surprising. First of all, it quickly became apparent that the fields long believed to be the realm of the Chinese—laundries, restaurants, and garment shops—while still a source of employment, were engaging a smaller percentage of the population than ever. Second, the patterns of immigration had shifted not just in the staggering increase in numbers but also in the background and gender of those coming into the country. In the first decades, Chinese immigrants had been almost exclusively men. Ever since the War Brides Act went into effect in 1946, the majority were women. In addition, an increasing number of Chinese immigrants were coming to America with advanced education and marketable skills. The Chinese had long started easing out of the lines of work to which they had once been relegated—washing and ironing, cooking and service—and into other, more esteemed fields. My research found that the years from the 1940 census to that of 1970 had witnessed a phenomenal increase in the Chinese in America working in professional and technical careers—from just 2.8 percent in 1940 to 26.5 percent in 1970.

I found that the percentage of Chinese women who were employed was higher than the national average, even before taking into account unpaid workers in family-run restaurants, groceries, and laundries who would likely not classify themselves as employed. I knew from experience how very many women fell into this unrecognized category of work.

Among those with official employment, nearly one in seven Chinese women in America worked as seamstresses—and fully half in New York City worked in garment factories. Disturbingly, I found that the median income of Chinese women in America was about half of that of Chinese males—a seemingly insurmountable discrepancy and a terrible reflection of women's compensation. This was particularly true because those men of Chinese descent who were earning close to double women's income were themselves notably underpaid in the wider labor market.

I could closely relate to these women who had the odds stacked against them in the labor market. As a child, I had watched my mother work alongside my father for long hours in our family's laundry, and I, too, had ironed clothes and bedding every single day to help make the family business profitable. As a young mother, I had passed up opportunities for professional growth because my first obligation was to my husband and my children. As a divorced mother of four, I had worked part time in various capacities, and I fully understood that my role in those jobs was not to do three- or four-days' worth of work but rather to do a full week's work in three- or four-days' time.

One of the most egregious instances of discrimination I'd encountered occurred when I applied for a position at a local university institute. The job called for someone who spoke a Far Eastern language, and the duties were to arrange the itineraries of Far Eastern scholars invited to the university to give lectures or attend symposia. I was fully qualified for this job and eager to apply. The employment agency and then the personnel office were impressed with my background. They sent me to meet the institute's director. The director reviewed my qualifications and interviewed me for some time. It seemed I had the job, but then he asked, "By the way, are you married?" I said I was, and he asked, "Do you have children?" I said I did. The last question was "How many?"

Apparently, my answer to that question cut me irrevocably out of the running for the job. Rather than offer me the position, the director gave me a fatherly admonition to stay home and take care of my children who needed me.

As I culled the statistics about women of Chinese descent who were working in greater proportion than any other group but being paid a fraction of what their male peers earned, I was angry on their behalf and determined to ensure their plight was represented in the study.

CRRO

One of the other major findings of this study was proof that a substantial portion of those from China or born to parents from China were underemployed. In some individual cases it was possible to identify that this was attributable to racism. In some it seemed due to cultural differences that handicapped the Chinese job applicant.

One of these differences is the cultural value the Chinese place on humility. This is a prized virtue in Chinese culture, but it is a heavy yoke when it comes to competing for a job in America, where the tactic of promoting one's educational background, personal qualities, experience, and abilities is a key part of winning a desired position.

Another barrier for any foreign-born immigrant is language, but for those coming from China, this barrier can seem insurmountable. While many European languages share a great deal of common ground with English words and grammar structure, making it possible to make some intuitive leaps in bridging the language barrier, there is no such commonality between Chinese and English languages. Everything—letters, word roots, pronunciation rules, sentence structure—is completely different, and so without ready and intensive instruction in learning their host country's language, many Chinese are doomed to face the language barrier for the rest of their lives.

In my interviews and research, I found many examples of a "glass ceiling" that was met by those of Chinese descent as well. I had encountered this firsthand when I'd worked at the Voice of America. I'd recommended a deserving colleague for promotion and was reminded that the list of qualifications demanded the successful applicant be a US citizen. I pointed out that this Chinese American applicant was, in fact, a native-born American. The hiring manager looked at me sheepishly and said, "You know what I mean." I did know. He meant that the ideal applicant would need to be white.

My brother Milton had also experienced limitations because of his ethnic background. After World War II, Milton earned a degree in aeronautical engineering and got hired at NASA. After a dozen years of diligent work and increasing responsibilities—no instrument left on a flight without his okay—he realized that while many of the engineers he trained were promoted up the chain of command, he had been overlooked for every promotion. Frustrated and unable to get answers from his superiors, Milton filed a Freedom of Information Act inquiry—and discovered that no Asian in NASA had ever been promoted beyond his entry level. His lawyer told him it was an open-and-shut case, and when Milton finally had a hearing, NASA promoted him two levels on the spot. Once promoted, he was treated coldly by his fellow employees and was uncomfortable in the hostile work environment. He applied for a job at McDonnell Douglas, and they quickly hired him at twice his NASA salary.

Few people raised in a home that values Chinese tradition would fight for a promotion like Milton did. He waited 12 years before he took action. The idea of demanding to be recognized goes against nearly everything the culture values. I was proud of my brother, though, for standing up for himself.

CREC

For each notable aspect of my research, I included a summary of the statistical points, graphs to exhibit the data, and my recommendations for how problem areas might be addressed. I also included personal anecdotes, stories of people I had read about or met, and quotations from other sources. I'd been told by some of my colleagues that my writing in *Mountain of Gold* was not sufficiently academic to represent the work of a professor, and so I tried to make the writing in the Manpower study more detached and official. I found, though, that I hated the more formal style, so I went back to telling stories and doing my best to present relatable characters and examples to animate the facts and research.

Cynthia was a dedicated and invaluable help to me throughout the Manpower project. She created many of the tables in the book and typed the final manuscript. Later, when she applied for a summer job in Great Neck, her typing test showed that she could type at an error-free rate of 70 words per minute. Her would-be employer was delighted and wanted to hire her right away, but on closer inspection of Cynthia's application, he realized she was only 16—and child labor laws dictated she was underage to work the required hours.

Prager Press accepted *Chinese American Manpower and Employment* for publication in 1975, and the following year it was recognized with a Best Book for 1976 award from *Choice Magazine*—the academic equivalent of *Publishers Weekly*.

The highest and best recognition I received for this book did not come from an award or a review, though. It arrived the day my phone rang and I found myself speaking with the head of the Manpower Administration. He told me he had just finished the book after reading it all day, and he wanted me to know that because he'd found it so informative and valuable, he was ordering 500 copies to send to other agencies and administrators in the federal government.

CB&C

With the Manpower study completed, I turned to another project. At the request of a group of New York City teachers who were struggling to handle the influx of immigrant children from China, I began researching the challenges kids have to overcome as they start schools where both their language and culture are not the norm.

During the early months of my investigation, though, the thing that demanded attention was a palpable fear in the community. That year, 1976, was a period of great unrest in Chinatown. Crime was rampant, and arrests were rising. Parents escorted their children— even teenagers—to and from school. They forbade them from going outside to play. They installed one lock after another—often on rickety doors that would not withstand any kind of assault. They put bars on the windows of their homes and apartments, and even residents of new high-rise buildings were sometimes fearful of getting in the elevator or going to the laundry room. Too many of their neighbors had been mugged.

Out on the streets, things were no better. Many residents were afraid to go to the movies or out to eat. The streets of Chinatown that had once been a safe haven for Chinese immigrant families had become the disputed turf of rival gangs like the Ghost Shadows, the Flying Dragons, and the Black Eagles—and the gangs were tearing the community apart.

Frustrated by an inability to deal with the gangs and the Chinatown community's reluctance to report their activities, the state Office of Child Development and the Department of Health, Education, and Welfare asked me to create a report. They wanted to know how the gangs operated, who was joining them, and most importantly, how it might be possible to disrupt their recruiting and activities.

It was not an easy decision to help with this endeavor. I had eight children and could not risk exposing them to any danger. I knew how vicious the gangs could be. In Chinatown alone, there were 26 murders committed by gang members that year.

In the end, though, I agreed to look into it. This was a problem that had been kept hidden by almost everyone in Chinatown, and I believed that until it came to light, it was not going away.

In my research, I had ample opportunities to interview social workers, civic leaders, police officers, and former gang members. I found that many gang members were young men who did not speak English and were coming from a background of Communism. Finding themselves unable to succeed in school or get jobs, some of them joined gangs. These groups almost exclusively exploited other members of the Chinese community.

In addition to my other sources, I also set up an interview with active gang members, reassuring them that I was not interested in their identities or in them individually but rather in their experiences and opinions. On the day of the interview, I met these two young men at an apartment, and before they said a word, they searched every corner for hidden persons or recording equipment. Even after they were sure neither trap was waiting for them, they were nervous—constantly watching the door.

I finally started asking questions, leading off with a simple, "How old are you?"

Neither of them would say, but when I pressed for a reason, they gave me a lesson in American juvenile law. In short, the law protected those under 16, so no gang member would readily admit to being any older.

Both of the gang members were immigrants from Hong Kong, and both were high school dropouts. I had been able to set up the interview because one of them had been in my class for a time, and so he trusted me a bit. This boy had surprised me—his midterm score was the highest of all my students in his term. Shortly after the test, though, a policeman came to the college looking for him, alleging that this charming, handsome, intelligent boy had fired a gun at a group of people who got in his way when he tried to crash a private event. It was difficult to reconcile the two characters—the promising student and the brazen criminal—with one another.

I asked the young men how they'd gotten involved in the gangs and why they stayed, and their answers revolved solely around money. They had been recruited and given a steady income, and after that they'd been hooked. They talked about having been shot at and knifed and beaten up, but neither of them considered leaving the gang a possibility.

When I asked what the young men did with the money they made through their illegal dealings, one of them told me he sent $800 to his parents in Hong Kong each month, along with a letter telling them how hard he was studying in school in New York.

"If I quit," he said, "how can I face my parents with no education and no money? There's no way out for me."

At the end of the interview, the two boys asked me for $100 for their time, and since I thought they would take it from me anyway, I emptied out my purse. I only had about $30, which I handed over. They were disappointed, but they took the money and left.

In my report, I made recommendations for the police, the judicial system, the community, the neighborhood associations, the parents, and the schools. It was clear there was no one-step fix for the gang problem in Chinatown, but neither was it insurmountable. The essence of the problem was that young men who were unproductive, unsupervised, uneducated, and adrift in the community could be corrupted by opportunists who saw they could be easily manipulated for money.

The solution needed to include a stronger police presence, deportation for gang leaders, and prosecution for repeat offenders. It also required that the community acknowledge and face the gang problem, rather than continue to try to cover it up and keep it as Chinatown's dirty secret. Most of all, I pointed out that if these youths had been actively engaged in jobs, in schoolwork supported by bilingual education, and in other activities, most would never have gotten involved in gangs in the first place.

When I'd finished my research, an editor at the *New York Times Magazine* asked me if I'd write an article about Chinatown gangs for the magazine, but I declined. I didn't want to put my family in danger. My research was published as a booklet for government agencies to use but was never released for public sale.

In time, the government did crack down on gang leaders by prosecuting or deporting them. The illegal gambling business that had helped foster and support gang activities mostly transferred to legal entities in Atlantic City and Foxwood. Over time, the gangs that had terrorized Chinatown during the 1970s were largely eradicated.

In the long run, some of the boys I knew to be gang members during that time became upstanding, contributing members of the Chinatown community. Those young men and the people of Chinatown have put this dark period of the past behind them.

ℭℬ ℬ

Chapter 13

BURIED HISTORY

The early years after I married Charles, while we still had children at home, seem almost impossible for me to fathom now. I wonder at the pace we had to maintain and that we managed to take care of everyone that needed us and everything that needed to be done. Charles went to Kenya, Venezuela, and Iran for the UN, leading a delegation on the international law of the seas, as well as to countless other destinations for his own business. He was sometimes gone for months, and I managed the demands of our home, my job at City College, my research, and our eight children on my own.

At those times, I was like a single mom again, though now I had twice as many children to care for and keep safe. One particularly scary episode occurred when Calvin had a serious sledding accident while Charles was away working in Puerto Rico. Calvin lost control of his sled and went under a car, slicing a deep gash across his head. Alan ran home to tell me Calvin was bleeding profusely, and we called an ambulance to take him to the emergency room. I stayed up all night at the hospital by his side to make sure he didn't lose consciousness.

Our children made Charles and me very proud. They were growing up to be responsible, hardworking, and well grounded. In their academics, they were outstanding, excelling first in school and then, as they got older, at their universities. Some went on to graduate school and even one to medical school. The list of schools they attended would come to include Princeton, Cornell, U Penn, Wharton, Columbia, Yale, Brandeis, MIT, George Washington, and others. Across the board, they got good grades and scholarships.

The children blended together into one big, cooperative family and spent birthdays, holidays, graduations, and other special occasions together—even as the older ones started establishing families of their own. As they spread out across the country, they continued to visit each other's homes and vacation together. Charles and I were so proud of our model blended family. It sometimes felt as if the children had always been together.

It sometimes felt like Charles and I had always been together, too. I felt completely secure in our marriage. He admired and depended on me, and I admired and trusted him. We went about our days knowing that when life stopped being so terribly busy, we'd have time to enjoy it together.

CRBD

In the meantime, though, there was a great deal of work to be done. I had been approached by a group of public school teachers who were puzzled. The few Chinese students they'd taught in the past had always been quiet, humble, and diligent workers. Now they were welcoming large numbers of new immigrants from China in their classes, and these students were struggling to adjust to the classroom as well as to the work. Teachers didn't know how to handle these students, and a few asked if I could help. My classes at City College had been profiled in an article in the *New York Times* in 1972, and some combination of that publicity and my ongoing work in the field of Chinese immigrant assimilation had brought them to me.

Part of the problem was well known to anyone familiar with Chinese culture and politics. For hundreds of years, scholarship was greatly prized and respected in China. Schooling was not free, so it carried the esteem that comes with being an entity that is valued but difficult to attain. Men like Charles and my first husband, Bill, were considered the best and brightest of their generation—so much so that they were chosen to come to the United States to earn advanced degrees. There were few positions so respected as that of the scholar in those days.

Mao Tse-Tung's takeover of the government and imposition of Communism changed all that. His regime placed little value on scholars. His doctrine dictated that educated young people "go the countryside to be reeducated by the ... peasants." Scholars who wanted to go their own way and those who dared speak against the Communist government were dealt with summarily.

Cynthia discovered firsthand how the Chinese government squelched free thought and kept close control on education. She had always shared my interest in Chinese culture and history, and after she graduated from Yale in 1980, she was selected by the Yale-China association to reestablish their program in mainland China—a program that had been suspended when the Communists came to power. And so it happened that just as China was emerging from the devastation of the Cultural Revolution, Cynthia traveled there to spend two years teaching at Wuhan University. Despite her substantial education and exposure to the politics and practices in China, Cynthia was accustomed to the openness of American education and went into her overseas experience thinking she could teach her students American folk songs and share American holiday traditions like Valentine's Day and Halloween with them. She quickly found herself closely monitored and under suspicion, but she stuck it out, teaching English and American history classes until the end of her assignment.

Under Mao's leadership, children were offered a minimal education, always coupled with labor, so it was no wonder that the immigrant students who came from China to America in the 1970s were quite different from those of earlier decades. The doctrines implemented in 1949 had taken root. The new immigrants came from a world where advanced learning and critical thought had long been actively discouraged at every level. Imbued with this cultural background of disrespect for education, large numbers of these new students created mayhem for American teachers.

I was able to offer the teachers some political and cultural perspective, and I also began researching the unique hardships of transplanted Chinese children in New York. I began to consider, from an academic perspective, how wrenching it must be for an immigrant child to find his or her cumulative life experiences completely invalidated in a new country and new school—how impossible it must seem to realize that it is not just a whole new set of speech patterns that must be learned but a whole new system of behavior as well.

My siblings and I had been born to Chinese parents in an American city. We'd always had some exposure to both cultures. In both the United States and China, we were outsiders, but we were able to adapt and survive. Still, I could well imagine how difficult it must be for children who had only experienced one culture and one language to suddenly be forced to function in another.

I analyzed a number of different aspects of cultural difference—including aggressiveness, sexuality, demonstration of affection, education, respect for parental authority, and individualism—in terms of how the cultural experience of the children might create conflict as they assimilated.

In one example, I looked at how very differently Chinese and American cultures view aggression. In Chinese culture, the soldier, or the man who resorts to violence, stands on the lowest rung of the social ladder. A scholar or gentleman achieves things by his wits, not his fists. A child is taught all his life that he demeans himself and his family if he fights.

An American child, on the other hand, may have a different relationship with aggression. Most parents will not encourage it, but neither will they insist their children turn the other cheek. American popular culture idolizes the underdog who fights back and wins, and it castigates those who would avoid conflict at all costs.

When the Chinese child encounters bullying and intimidation at school, he becomes an easy victim with no way out that will sit well with both his classmates and parents. If he defends himself, he fails his parents; if he continues to be a victim, he'll be disrespected by his peers. There is no solution that respects the priorities of both the culture in which he was raised and the one in which he wishes to assimilate.

Another common conflict I found had to do with how parents demonstrate affection. Traditional Chinese parents aren't big on hugs and kisses and outspoken proclamations of fondness. In Chinese culture, these expressions are not the norm. This has nothing to do with whether Chinese parents love their children—of course they do—but it is how family members are raised to relate to one another.

Imagine an immigrant child who comes to New York in the third or fourth grade and begins to assimilate into American culture. All around her, that child sees parents who openly and frequently embrace their children. On television and at the movies, she sees families where fathers and mothers say things like "I'm so proud of you" and "I love you" to their children. What is the Chinese child, newly introduced to this culture, to think? Too often, she may begin to wonder whether she is loved at all, and that insecurity will contribute to her overall difficulty with assimilating into her new school and new group of friends. It'll also lead to conflicts with her parents down the line.

I found that teachers and parents were often unaware of these cultural conflicts and that they sometimes ascribed inaccurate

meanings or motives to children's behavior as a result. As a result of my research, I wrote an article titled "Bicultural Conflict," which was published in four or five journals and magazines. I also wrote a book titled *Transplanted Chinese Children*. I used the topic for my doctoral thesis. After that, it was published by the Center for Migration Studies.

In 1986, after earning a Ph.D. for my research and writing on this subject, I was promoted to full professor at City College.

☙☞

All around me during this time, there were Chinese parents who were distressed that their children were dating non-Chinese boys and girls. In addition, I saw that many of my students were dating outside their cultures and keeping it a secret from their parents. Intermarriage was not legal in many American states until the Supreme Court ruled against miscegenation laws in 1967. Even after the practice became legal in all 50 states, it was still taboo in many families and communities—both those of long-established Americans and those of immigrants. But immigration had never been so prolific and from such varied places on the globe as it became after 1965, so perhaps the uptick in intermarriages was inevitable.

There was no data available about intermarriage of Asians for anyone to cite—but there were plenty of questions about whether these unions were socially acceptable, whether they were advisable, and whether they could even work in the long term.

I decided to tackle the issue. City hall kept records of everyone who got married, and each license was notated with the ethnicity of the bride and groom and their parental backgrounds. I believed this information could provide me with all the data I needed, but no one had access to it except the city clerk. I had to get the consent of the city clerk, David Dinkins (who would later become the mayor of New York). I was told that I was only the second person ever granted this privilege, and I had to swear to keep the information I uncovered about individuals private.

Each borough kept its own records separately and on paper, so I had to travel to all five boroughs to obtain the data for New York

City alone. I thumbed through thousands upon thousands of forms for the years 1972 and 1982, looking for the ethnicity of each bride and groom to see if either was Chinese.

This process, along with US Census data, gave me numbers, indicating that the rate of out-marriage from the Chinese community in New York was 15 to 17 percent. The numbers did not tell me anything, though, about the inner workings of these marriages. I decided to interview 50 couples to hear their stories. Finding willing participants was more difficult than I'd imagined. This was a sore subject for many people, as some children had been disowned and ostracized from their families and communities for falling in love with someone of a different ethnic background.

Not surprisingly, the interviews revealed that family objection posed the most significant problems in these intermarriages. All kinds of obstructionist tactics had been brought to bear by the families to block the unions of my interview subjects. This was a group who had survived the ordeal, though, and ultimately married, and perhaps their us-against-them outlooks had solidified their relationships. Overall, the couples reported few problems in their marriages due to cultural, language, or religious differences. Their complaints were mainly in the area of personal habits of the spouse—complaints no different than those in any other marriage.

As a result of my research, I published a book titled *Chinese American Intermarriage* in 1990 and wrote several articles in journals and magazines about the subject.

My research into intermarriage was a fascinating study to me, in part because this topic impacted families all around me as well as my own. Four of the eight children in our family married non-Chinese spouses. After the publication of *Chinese American Intermarriage*, though, I decided that researching and writing for publication was getting too laborious for me. Little did I know that the next topic to capture my interest would be perhaps the most important, interesting, and laborious discovery of my career.

Most scholars of this time had long assumed that Chinese immigrants first came to the West Coast of North America and then made their way across the country to the east in the 1870s and later—after the completion of the Transcontinental Railroad. That said, recorded history shows that Chinese labor was imported into Peru, Cuba, and other parts of South America long before the Gold Rush in California. I wanted to know whether some of these immigrants might have come to the East Coast of the United States in earlier years.

Sniffing here and there, I learned that the National Archives had some old immigration records stashed at a warehouse on a pier in Bayonne, New Jersey. No one seemed to know anything about these records, so I drove out to have a look. The pier jutted out into the Atlantic Ocean, and the attendant who opened up the building and turned on the lights for me said the records had never been consulted before. Hundreds of boxes of immigrations files had been stacked from floor to ceiling in the warehouse for as long as anyone could remember. Once, the attendant confessed, one of the workers had even proposed dumping the seemingly useless reams of paper into the ocean.

Luckily they didn't. I asked the attendant for the earliest box. His reply: "Help yourself." There was no known order or system to the files and no way to tell which was oldest or most recent. I opened the nearest box and pulled out one file and then another. My eyes got wide, and my heart started to pound: these were the files of Chinese immigrants who had come through East Coast ports as early as 1860. They predated the time the Chinese supposedly first came east, after the completion of the Transcontinental Railroad, by a decade.

As I rifled through the boxes, I was struck by another unexpected element of the files. These were not just forms; the paperwork was lengthy and detailed, with pages of notes, photographs, and other documents. I headed straight back to City College and wrote out grant requests to two funding sources: one to the Chiang Ching Kuo Foundation, a Taiwan-based organization that provides grants for research on Chinese studies, and one to the National Endowment for the Humanities. I proposed to put the files in a database for future researchers and genealogists. I pointed out the invaluable nature of the files for descendants of the people documented there. Imagine how they might feel, discovering they could lay hands on the files and find photos and detailed records of their ancestors. The photographs in the files alone were priceless.

Both foundations granted me funds, and I had all 581 boxes moved to the National Archive in Manhattan, where I could easily access them to begin my work. There was no discernible order to the way they had gone to storage. Certainly they were not organized by any obvious marker like name or date. Much later, I would discover that the boxes had been filed according to which ship the immigrants arrived on, but at the time, the system by which they were stored was a mystery.

A typical file was several pages long and contained identification cards, exit permits from China, entry applications to the United

States, witness information about the immigrant, a photograph of the applicant, and, in some cases, supplemental family photographs, postcards, telegrams, and certificates. In addition, as I dug deeper in the files, I found that many contained transcripts of immigration interviews with the applicants. During the decades these files were accumulated, a typical Chinese entrant into America was detained by immigration, much like a prisoner, for months. In their suspicion of the Chinese and their efforts to ferret out paper sons, immigration officials interrogated these men (you could almost count the female applicants on your fingers, there were so few) at great length about their personal histories, their villages, their voyages—in short, anything that might reveal them to be someone other than the person their papers suggested.

The result of all this documentation is a depiction of Chinese immigration history unlike anything that had ever been discovered before. The files revealed rigorous, often intimidating questioning. Immigration officials probed everything from what livestock a family had owned in China to details of the village square or the number of stairs in a home. They compared the answers to these questions to those given by previous respondents and would immediately deport anyone who gave answers that didn't match up.

The files brought the struggles and sometimes painful bullying and racist immigration procedures of the past to light, and I believed my work digging through all those boxes and files would one day make the information in them available to anyone who wanted to know the truth.

There were times when the work was infuriating or tragic, such as in the cases of immigrants held in detention for years and the records of those who committed suicide because of the oppressive pressure or eventual rejection for entry.

In the cases of those who were admitted into the country, the files often documented follow-up visits by immigration officials, and these provide a remarkable snapshot of the Chinese immigrant experience—capturing information like where the entrants were residing, how they were making a living, and whether they had connected with extended family members.

In my eyes, after spending decades researching and writing about the Chinese immigrant experience, the social history contained in those 581 boxes was nothing short of remarkable.

In an effort to establish an order for the information, I created a standardized form that could be used to document every individual. There was room for three spellings of a person's name, taking into account that it could be spelled different ways and that the surname in Chinese always preceded the given name. There was room for the Chinese characters if a person came in under false pretense as a "paper son." If there were photos in the file, the form would indicate this. In this way, anyone could search the database for information. However, to view the actual photos or to see the contents of the file, one had to go to the archive to view it in person.

∞

In 1992, after 22 years at City College, I retired from teaching. I did not go quietly to my rocking chair but further immersed myself in assessing and recording the massive document find from New Jersey. It was painstaking work making a file for each person and doing what I could to ensure it could be found if someone came looking for it.

I hired two retired men who lived in my building to help me sort through the files, and their assistance was vital in getting the work done. Because both had lived long lives as part of New York's Chinatown, some days they came across names and records of people they knew, or had known as children, in the boxes.

It took three years—until 1995—to completely catalog the Bayonne files. In some ways, because technology kept galloping forward, the project was more complicated than it would have been a decade earlier or a decade later. First, I put all the information on file cards, but when I asked what would happen when the cards were gone, it was suggested the data be saved on microfiche tape. By the time that transfer was done, I was informed that the tapes would eventually disintegrate, and the data would be safer on computer disks.

I'm not entirely sure all the formats in which the data is available today (I believe they are available on Ancestry.com), but I do know that I had to fight to keep the original paper files in New York. Much later, after the devastation of September 11, 2001, the Immigration Service wanted to move the files to a storage facility in Colorado, but it was important to me that they be accessible to people who were researching their family members. I had cataloged all the information in the boxes so as to make it possible for anyone who cared to look to be able to find the correct box and file for their ancestor or the subject of their research. In the end, wiser heads prevailed, and the files remained in the National Archives in Lower Manhattan, easily accessible from Chinatown and anywhere else in New York.

The announcement that the archiving was complete generated national and international media interest. *Humanities* magazine ran a multipage feature article called "Paper Sons" about the files, and several newspapers, including *The New York Times, The Seattle Times,* and *The Los Angeles Times,* published articles about the project and my findings. One journalist wrote:

> *The records expose a time when American immigration*
> *officials' questions were personal and insulting;*
> *others were excruciating in precision.*
> *Does your mother have bound feet? How many homes are located*
> *in your native village? How many windows are in each room*
> *of your home? Which direction does the village stream flow?*
> *How many male and female water buffalo do you own?*
> *Immigration officials judged the body language of applicants,*
> *looking for perspiration or nervousness. Stuttered and*
> *stammered responses often resulted in deportation.*
> *Betty Lee Sung, professor emerita of history at the City*
> *College of New York, hopes the project will help exhume*
> *and rewrite a buried part of American history.*

I did, indeed, hope to set the record straight and believed creating a database of the 12,000 files would open up a new interest in an accurate depiction of the Chinese immigration experience. The National Endowment for the Humanities, which had provided one of the grants that made my work possible, asked me to take on the job of cataloging the records for all 12 entry ports into the United States, but I was 71 years old then. Considering my family obligations and the pace at which I'd been working for so many years, I felt tackling the New York files would have to be enough. The remaining

11 ports would have to wait until someone else got a grant to tackle them. To date, no one has.

CRⁿꝘꓫꙄ

I had barely finished working on the Bayonne files when, in the spring of 1996, a city councilwoman from Flushing, Queens, was quoted in *The New York Times* after making disparaging remarks about the changing ethnic makeup of her district. She depicted Asians as criminal smugglers and rude merchants, and she categorized immigration in her district as "an invasion, not assimilation."

I may have been retired, but I would have had to be comatose to let that kind of comment pass without rebuttal. As one of the city's authorities of Asian American history and relations, I had to respond. I was interviewed by the *Times* for an answer to these demeaning and deeply disappointing comments from a politician I knew and had respected, and then I turned my attention to helping organize a rally at city hall to make sure the Asian American community of New York had its voice heard by the councilwoman and those who would follow her lead. I agreed to be the emcee for this event as well.

I found it a sad commentary on the state of gender equality in the Chinese community, though, that on the morning of the rally, the president of Chinese Consolidated Benevolent Association called me to tell me he did not want the event to be led by a woman. He asked me to step down and allow the executive director of the association to speak in my place. Reluctantly, to keep the peace on a day when our community needed to show solidarity, I gave this gentleman half my notes, and we shared the podium.

Despite this setback, the event was a success. The rally drew thousands of protestors, including Mayor Giuliani, Governor Pataki, and New York residents from all different walks of life and ethnic backgrounds. After the rally, the councilwoman apologized in front of the city council.

My son Victor tells the story of taking the subway from his job in midtown to get to city hall. As he emerged from the subway onto the street, he recalls being a little confused about exactly which way he should walk to get to the event. He asked a policeman for directions, but before the officer could answer, Victor heard my voice, from blocks away, being broadcast over a public address system. He thanked the policeman, told him, "Never mind," and proceeded to follow the sound of my voice to the rally.

Leading a rally against Councilwoman Harrison.
City Hall, NYC, 1996.

Even as I stepped away from the academic world, I continued to worry about the longevity of the Asian American studies program to which I had devoted so many years of work. I wanted to make sure the department would go on and that the research I had started in places like the Lawrence Radiation Lab at Berkeley, New York's city hall, and the Bayonne pier would be the beginning of a much greater body of information and understanding about Asian Americans. I hoped someone would pick up where I had left off to investigate the same kinds of statistics for Asian groups other than the Chinese, as well as for emerging demographic groups like intermarried couples and their children and the many children adopted from Asia after the Korean and Vietnam wars.

Unfortunately, shortly after I left, the Asian Studies Department was abolished, with some courses going to the History Department and Mandarin to the Modern Language Department. Despite New York City's having a 14 percent Asian American population in 2015, only one college, Hunter, offers a few courses in Asian American studies. It is some consolation that while the offerings in New York have dwindled, hundreds of Asian American studies courses have sprung up in colleges and universities throughout the country,

Even though I had retired from City University, I lobbied the administrators to establish an institute that would support my goals. The Asian American/Asian Research Institute (AAARI) was established in November of 2001 and continues to serve as a university-wide scholarly research and resource center that focuses on policies and issues that affect Asians and Asian Americans.

For some time, I served as the chair of the board of directors for the institute, but in more recent years, I have passed the reins on to younger scholars with their own ideas for its success. The institute is a legacy I hope will carry on for generations.

Over the years of my career, I collected research materials related to every subject about which I wrote. In my retirement, I found myself surrounded by my sizable collection of books, newspapers, brochures, photographs, clippings, and all the other documents that comprise a scholar's paper trail. I suspected that some of the documents might be rare or of historical value, and I hoped they might provide useful source material for researchers who would follow me in the field of Asian American studies.

Years before my retirement, I'd learned that when members of the United States Congress need research or information, their staffs rely largely on the collections in the Library of Congress. I remembered all too well the hair-raising contents of the library's very limited materials about Chinese Americans from my days researching for Voice of America, and so I approached Hwa Wei Lee, chief of the Asian Division, about donating my papers there. He proposed my donation to Congress, and they approved it.

I sent 53 cartons of collected research materials to the Library of Congress, where they were added as the "Betty Lee Sung Collection" to the Asian Reading Room. The library described the collection as "a microcosm of the Asian American experience," and Dr. Lee said the Library of Congress considered my materials "one of the most valuable research resources available on the subject."

I was happy to know that my papers would be preserved and made available to future students and researchers.

CR ꝰↄ

Chapter 14

A TIME FOR FAMILY

A t the end of the archival project, my family urged me to take a rest from the hectic pace I'd been maintaining for decades. Though I continued to be involved in community and academic organizations, this was a time for Charles and me to enjoy together. Our children were grown, and we were now proud grandparents. We had enough money and time to travel, and we could choose our adventures. Rose advised us to treat this time as our "golden days," and we took her counsel to heart.

In March of 1998, we celebrated Charles's eightieth birthday surrounded by our big, beautiful family. Our family portrait reflects the happiness of the day, with many of the adults holding toddlers and babies in our arms and everyone smiling at our many blessings.

For Charles and me, traveling was the best way to enjoy our newfound freedom. In the early years of our marriage, I had found that traveling with Charles when he was working was not as much fun as I'd imagined it would be. When we were first married, he asked if I wanted to go to Puerto Rico, and I jumped at the chance. When we got there, though, Charles rented a car and appointed me as his driver and chief navigator. There was no GPS then—just maps! I quickly learned that I did not want to go along on his business trips. In our shared retirement, however, we were able to travel for pleasure.

We bought a small co-op in Florida, right across the hall from the one Rose and Arthur had purchased years before. During the coldest months of the winter, we'd close up our apartment in New York and head south, where we could sit out on the balcony and see and smell the ocean within view. We lived there each year from January through March, soaking up the sun and swimming in the pool downstairs. We visited our children, who by then were scattered on both coasts and beyond. We relished the time we had with our grandchildren, who seemed to be getting older by the minute.

I traveled to China with Tina and her husband, Harry, in 1995 to help out as a guide, translator, and grandmother when they adopted one of our granddaughters there. Cynthia, too, adopted two girls from China. This was around the time China's one-child policy was enacted, and these precious infant girls had been abandoned by families who wanted their one child to be a son.

During our early retirement years, Charles and I visited big cities and small towns, as well as natural wonders like the Grand Canyon and Bryce Canyon. Somewhere I even have a photograph of the two of us grinning happily as we plunged down the river on a white-water rafting trip.

We went on a lot of cruises, sometimes traveling with Rose and Arthur or with one or more of the children. We sailed to Alaska, where we saw the Hubbard Glacier and the snow-capped mountains of the Inside Passage. We went all over the Caribbean—I believe we took at least ten cruises there. On these trips, Charles was able to do some scouting for his business, and I inquired on our tours about Chinese immigration to each new area. When we went to Aruba, I asked our guide if there were any Chinese families on the island, and she laughed and said, "Are you kidding me? The Chinese own this island!" Then she pointed out the supermarkets and restaurants owned by Chinese inhabitants.

In 2002, Charles received an invitation to attend a reunion of the alumni from his police college. It was to be held in Bangkok, Thailand. We traveled there together, and since Charles and I were both adventuresome, we saw as much as possible. We visited the Grand Palace that has been the home of the kings of Siam since the 1700s, toured a snake farm where venom is extracted from dozens of different breeds to create antivenom, and toured an elephant preserve. The highlight of this trip, though, was our visit to a tiger farm. There, we saw tigers being suckled by mother pigs. I saw a man washing windows in a room where more than a dozen tigers were roaming freely. I would have been terrified in his position, but he went about his job nonchalantly, as if there were no chance at all that any of those giant predators might harm him.

Charles and Betty at the tiger farm in Thailand.

Outside the main building of the farm, there was one tiger chained to a tree stump. A photographer asked if anyone wanted to take a picture with it. Everyone in our group hesitated, but I couldn't stand to let the opportunity pass. I said, "*Yes.* I want a picture!" Charles joined me, and we were both photographed with the huge, beautiful animal. Before we moved on, I asked if I could pet the tiger, and when I did, it purred like a cat.

Before coming home from Thailand, Charles and I toured South Vietnam. We saw some of the US military equipment that still remained in the country, as well as the tunnels the Vietnamese dug so that they could move about the country concealed from foreign forces. I thought about all the turmoil my students had felt and expressed over the war in Vietnam and wondered what good had come of it.

Another favorite trip Charles and I took during our shared retirement was a cruise to Australia and New Zealand. In addition to seeing the Great Barrier Reef and coastal areas of Australia, we went inland to Ayers Rock, which the local people call *Uluru*. This gigantic monolith juts out of the desert and is like nothing else I've seen in the world. We all had to wear net hoods over our faces and bodies to protect us from the swarms of flies at the rock. The native Aborigines who live in the desert were used to the flies, though, and didn't even react when they buzzed across their faces and around their eyes.

Helicoptor ride over Australia.

Along the coast, we met a group of Australian Maoris. They "adopted" Charles as one of their own and exchanged the *Hongi* greeting with him. This gesture, where two parties press their foreheads and noses together at the same time, supposedly makes an outsider one of the people of the land by sharing the breath of life with them.

When we got to New Zealand, it seemed there were more sheep than people. Everyone was so hospitable—we were even invited to a stranger's home for dinner. The countryside was beautiful—I believe we saw more waterfalls there than in all the other places we'd been to together.

I am grateful for the happiness and adventures of those years. That time, when we went about our days as old married couples do, thinking we would always have such ease and good fortune, was not destined to last.

Chapter 15

TRAGEDY STRIKES

In October of 2004, our whole family gathered at an elegant Chinese restaurant in the World Financial Center in Manhattan to celebrate my 80th birthday. For the occasion, my children, grandchildren, and many former colleagues and students sent letters, which my daughters had bound into a book. The letters were a moving testament to the first eight decades of my life. Charles wrote a letter for everyone to read that recounted our courtship and his repeated proposals. He wrote about how I had taken good care of him over the decades of our marriage, making sure he ate well and dressed well. He told me to enjoy the love of our eight children, their spouses, and our grandchildren.

All the children wrote letters about important moments in our lives together and some about how they viewed my career. One of my favorite notes came in Tina's letter, when she recounted watching a ceremony that had recognized my work earlier that year. I had received a Pioneer Award in Boston from the National Organization of Chinese Americans. During the ceremony, they played a video about my life's work. Tina wrote that the crowd had chanted for me to make a speech, and as I'd made my way to the podium, everyone got to their feet. "Miya looked at me with shining eyes and said, 'Wow, Grandma is so important.'"

Pioneer Award, received in Boston from the National Organization of Chinese Americans.

I was delighted that my granddaughter would say such a thing.

Victor wrote about the mixed blessing of being known as "Betty's son" and of how proud he was of my accomplishments in our family and in my career.

Cynthia wrote about how walking through Chinatown with me and meeting all the people who came up to reminisce about my classes or to discuss the goings-on in the community made the big, impersonal city feel like a small town.

Cathie thanked me for "the happiness and love, which you bring to my father and the care and attention that you have given him."

Calvin, the youngest of the children, wrote about how he'd been so proud as a little boy that his mother had written a book—he asked everyone he met if they knew me. In the small world of the neighborhood where we lived, nearly everyone did know me, not as an author but as the mother of eight children who lived in the community.

Calvin thanked me for all the things I taught him and for being a role model for him and for all the children.

Wilma wrote, "I now know how difficult your job was as the head of our household. You worked hard to teach us and guide us. You were our mom to whom we turned for assistance in dealing with the trials and tribulations of our respective lives. You were there to heal our wounds and relieve our frustrations."

On that day, there were no divisions in our family. After nearly four decades of marriage, Charles and I viewed all the children and grandchildren as "ours" together, despite the fact that we had once been two separate families.

Cঃৰৎড

Charles and I had been happily married for 37 years, but things were changing. Charles had always been absentminded in a way that was part of his charm, but in 2003 he became forgetful and oddly aggressive about it. His personality was changing. This was so unlike him. Charles was always an easygoing, relaxed man.

For years, his symptoms were mostly small things, but in 2003 Charles was diagnosed with Alzheimer's disease, and his illness changed his personality almost completely. He had always loved to watch basketball games on television, but as he got sicker, he wasn't interested. He'd made a decades-long habit of chatting on the phone with his friends each day, but when he became ill, he stopped making calls. At times, he was belligerent and confrontational, sometimes for no discernible reason—as if someone had offended him, even if nothing had been said. Now he would blame me when he misplaced his wallet, his credit cards, his bank book, or his eyeglasses.

My kind and trusting husband became suspicious and guarded, and even though he sometimes behaved like his "old" self, at other times it felt like I was living with a completely different person from the man I married.

The children were living all around the country, and so most of the time, it was just Charles and me in New York. At first, the disease only manifested itself in small ways, but as it progressed, his care became more difficult. His body, along with his mind, was weakening.

It was a difficult time in our lives, but we managed as best we could. After a long, happy marriage of so many years, I knew we would get through it.

Over the holidays in December of 2008, we took what would be our last trip together. Charles's niece and nephew were living in Honolulu, and his niece had managed to bring her own parents, uncle and aunt, and sister from China. Charles's children also attended, and we spent an entire week in Hawaii, enjoying the company of the extended family.

On Mother's Day of 2009, I received cards and gifts from the children, including a handmade card and an outfit from Charles's eldest daughter. One month later, in June, she suggested I send Charles out to her in Los Angeles for a few weeks so I could have a rest from the constant demands of his care. I was grateful for this offer, and since three of the children lived near each other on the West Coast, I thought they would be able to share in the responsibilities of supporting Charles's needs. I put him on a plane, in the front row, with a flight attendant looking after him, and I was assured the family would meet him when his plane landed.

Since Charles left to visit his children in June 2009, my family has been split apart. I have not seen him but once since that day he was taken away. I am still Charles's lawful spouse, but neither I nor his close friends have been able to speak with him or contact him. I do not understand the full reasons why Charles did not return to me or our home in New York. I do not know what prompted his children to decide to split our family in half. I was stunned, sorrowful, and confused at this turn of events. For 37 years we were a model family, and then suddenly that family was gone.

Thankfully, my own children stood by me in my time of sorrow. They, too, were puzzled and pained at the tragic division in our family. For some time after 2009, I was involved in a series of long and complicated court actions to resolve this issue, for Charles's children had substituted themselves as beneficiaries and removed my name even from the will, the trust, and all his assets. They even accused me of "stealing from my husband." I am neither at liberty nor inclined to detail in these pages the specifics of these actions except to say I have come away deeply disillusioned with the court system. I was mentally, physically, and emotionally drained by my experience within it. During this ordeal, I rapidly lost my hearing. I had a bad fall that fractured my ankle. Even after it healed, I couldn't walk like I used to. I was haunted by the tragic break in my family.

Fearing for my health and well-being, my children told me to settle the court case and put it behind me, which I did.

When I consulted Rose, my ever-wise sister said, "Don't look backward. Prioritize what you want in life." Even as I strove to take this good advice, I often thought of Charles. I wondered whether he missed his books, his friends, the view from our apartment in New York, or my presence in his life. I hoped he was well cared for. I hated to think of him isolated from all that was familiar to him in his old age and illness.

With my children's encouragement, I chose to do what I have always done. I got back out in the Chinatown community where I still, after all these years of retirement, get stopped by former students who tap me on the shoulder and ask, "Do you remember me?" I don't remember most of them. I taught thousands of students when they were just 18 or 19, and now they are all ages up to their 50s and 60s.

In 2015, the Museum of Chinese Americans honored me with an award that recognized me as a community hero, and there, too, I encountered former students—many of whom have gone on to do great things. One of my students is the current head of the OCA in New York, the equivalent of the NAACP for Chinese Americans. One is a member of the New York City Council, and another sits on the San Francisco Board of Supervisors. One is an immigration judge, one is a judge in Honolulu, and another is chief justice of the New York State Supreme Court. One former student, who was a nurse in the army when he took my class, sends me a card each year on Mother's Day and on Christmas from his home in North Carolina. I don't know what I did to deserve the honor of his faithful remembrance, but those cards have taken on a special meaning for me during these years when my family has been through so much.

As I reclaimed my life, I was able to spend time with my sister and my friends and to witness the endeavors of my four children and six grandchildren. Their graduations and accomplishments and the way they conduct themselves are an honor to me and to the Sung tradition.

At the request of one of my granddaughters and with the encouragement of my children, I began to write about my childhood, my travels, and my career. Writing about my life has been an opportunity to reflect, to remember, and to consider the choices I made.

I cannot change the things that have happened to me. I came into this world as a girl no one expected to amount to much. Yet through the ordeals, the joys and triumphs, and the trials and sorrows of the first 90 years of my life, I became a scholar, an author, a professor, an activist, a mother, and a wife.

AUTHOR BIOGRAPHY

D r. Betty Lee Sung is a scholar, author, professor, and leading authority on the history and experience of the Chinese in America. Her journey from a childhood as the defiant second daughter of a poor immigrant family to becoming one of the leading authorities in Asian American studies is a story of courage, compassion, and determination. When her first book, *Mountain of Gold,* was published in 1967, it was a landmark work—the first-ever comprehensive and meticulously researched chronicle of Chinese immigration and assimilation in the United States.

Dr. Sung pioneered the Asian American studies program at the City College of New York in 1970, offering courses that were the first of their kind in the eastern United States. For the next 22 years, she taught at City College and played an integral role in the expansion of those first few select courses into a full academic department.

Dr. Sung is the author of eight other books, including *The Story of the Chinese in America,* Colliers (1971); *Chinese in America,* Macmillan (1973); *Survey of Chinese Manpower and Employment,* Praeger (1976); *Album of Chinese Americans,* Franklin Watts (1977); *Statistical Profiles of the Chinese in the United States,* Arno Press (1979); *Adjustment Experience of Chinese Immigrant Children in New York City,* Center for Migration Studies (1987); and *Chinese American Intermarriage,* Center for Migration Studies (1990). Two versions of *Mountain of Gold* have been translated into Chinese by Mainland China and Taiwan.

Dr. Sung's writings represent only one facet of her life's work as a tireless advocate for Chinese Americans. Throughout her career, she has been committed to giving voice and history to this group that was often demeaned and persecuted. She has brought even complex and sometimes dark elements of the Chinese immigration story to light when others might have left them in the shadows. In recognition of the significance of her work and her enduring commitment and service, Dr. Sung has received dozens of honors, awards, and grants. Among these are:

- Chinese Culture Award for Contributions to Chinese-American Relations, by the Chinese government,
- University of Illinois "Comeback Honoree" Distinguished Alumni Award,
- Asian Americans for Equality Dream of Equality Award,
- Asian American Higher Education Council Outstanding Contribution to Education Award,

- National Organization of Chinese Americans Chinese American Pioneer Award,
- Honoree for the Celebration of Women's History Month in Manhattan,
- Museum of Chinese Americans Community Hero Award,
- Certificate of Appreciation for her "contribution to the ongoing fight against hatred and intolerance in America" from the Southern Poverty Law Center, and
- Grants from the National Endowment for the Humanities and the Chiang Ching Kuo Foundation to analyze and organize a historically priceless trove of immigration documents she discovered in a New Jersey warehouse

Dr. Sung and her work have been featured in museum exhibits in the New York Historical Exhibition (2014–2015) and in the Shanghai World Exhibition (2006). She received an honorary doctor of letters degree from the State University of New York in Old Westbury. Dr. Sung donated a collection of her academic and personal documents to the United States Library of Congress—a collection that was recognized as the core of the library's Asian American collection. It has become a key resource for today's scholars in the field.

At the beginning of her career, Dr. Sung set out to correct a racist and inaccurate image of the Chinese in America, and over the course of the decades that followed, she has influenced and witnessed tremendous progress toward equality for women and Asian Americans. In recent years, she has come to understand how vulnerable the elderly can be to people who would take advantage of their frailty and naiveté. In her 90s, Dr. Sung has turned her attention to promoting elder rights.

In addition to her significant professional endeavors, Betty Lee Sung is most proud of her four intelligent, kind, loyal, and talented children—Tina, Victor, Cynthia, and Alan. She considers them her greatest accomplishment.

Victor, Betty, Tina, Cynthia at recent Crab Fest, 2015

Tina, Alan, Elizabeth, Victor, Kitty Young (cousin), Rose (sister), Cynthia, Janet at family get-together, 2014

Rose, Betty, 2014

9 781599 326108